LONDON
from the AIR

LONDON
from the AIR

Photographs by
JASON HAWKES
Text by
FELIX BARKER

EBURY
PRESS

DEDICATION

TO OUR PARENTS

ACKNOWLEDGEMENTS

We would like to thank Julian Shuckburgh for all his help with the concept of *London from the Air*;
and, for his help on the flying side, Mark Barry-Jackson at Aeromega Helicopters. We would also
like to thank Andrew Nurnberg, Peter Grenville-Grey and David Tansley for their help and
support.

JASON HAWKES AND TIM KENDALL
AERIAL IMAGES, 1992

Photographs on page 1: Big Ben; page 2: Trafalgar Square and surrounding areas; page 6: the
City at night, with the Lloyds building in the foreground and Tower Bridge in the distance.

Contents

INTRODUCTION

A s THEIR PLANE breaks through murky clouds over Heathrow Airport, the first view many passengers have of London is the uninspiring sight of a reservoir. On a routine flight touchdown is generally only minutes away, but if air traffic is heavy they may be delayed and taken on an unexpected jaunt over the city. Impatience is offset by the fun of spotting famous buildings from unusual viewpoints. 'Isn't that Syon House?' 'Oh look, Battersea Power Station!' 'There's Vauxhall Bridge.' 'No, Chelsea, I think.'

The trouble is that such flights are too brief. The plane cannot be stopped for a second look. Jason Hawkes alters this, and the aerial tour on which he takes us allows us to examine landmarks from above in detail. A great deal of the charm of his pictures comes from their informality. When he does provide a studied composition of a familiar landmark it is invariably superb, but I find myself more beguiled by his shots of places most other air photographers don't bother about. You get the feeling that, with his colleague Tim Kendall, Hawkes has flown at dawn and late evening, in high summer and snowy winter, to catch London off its guard.

Rows of dull suburban streets acquire a new interest. We start to wonder how and when they came to be built, who lives in them, and whether the regimentation has affected their owners' personalities. Hawkes's camera focuses on a mysterious wooded island in the Serpentine. Does anyone ever visit it? An East End Jewish cemetery is laid out with remorseless symmetry. A fairground that is probably rather tatty sparkles like an eastern bazaar. A geometry of circles turns out to be a sewage works. Sometimes Hawkes himself cannot remember exactly where he was or what caught his fancy. Much time has had to be spent with a magnifying glass and Ordnance Survey maps. Local history libraries have been badgered to identify perplexing buildings. Anyone who prides himself on knowing his London can have a good game spotting some of the more obscure places. An added bonus are some extraordinary patterns: combined with snow, yellow mists and gaunt silhouettes, topography is lifted into the sphere of art.

London changes fast. Even the most up-to-date survey needs constant revision. These pictures are sufficiently topical to show the newly completed Charing Cross Station; the final stages being made to the Queen Elizabeth II Bridge connecting Kent and Essex at Dartford and now open; the eccentric progress in Docklands. Views from different angles of Britain's highest building – the 800-foot Canary Wharf – are valuable as they capture the penultimate months of construction. Some views are prophetic. Look now – for this may be your last chance – on the waste ground between King's Cross and St Pancras stations. Soon it will be transformed into the Channel Tunnel terminus.

Because air photography has such a modern flavour, historical commentary may sometimes seem slightly incongruous. But, looking down on a palace with so rich a past as Hampton Court, the camera has the ability, not possible on the ground, of showing different ages simultaneously; and these need historical definition. The aerial camera is also able to spy on the past and reveal secrets. From above we have verification of how Wren built false outer walls round St Paul's. High above Westminster Abbey the plans of medieval craftsmen to build a central spire or tower become clear. What is that strange circular building off Leicester Square? Investigation reveals that the modern French church on the site has adopted the shape of an 18th-century rotunda which exhibited panoramas here. By peering from the air above Whitehall we see how a Victorian architect designing courtyards of a Treasury building was inspired by the 17th-century plans of Inigo Jones.

For those concerned with such matters, Jason Hawkes was shooting with a Pentax 645 with inbuilt light meter, on Kodak 220 EPN, using 150mm and 45mm lenses, and an 80-160 zoom. He and Kendall flew in a hired helicopter mostly at 700 to 800 feet, but sometimes going to 1,500 feet for wider angles. Shots were made from open doors at the sides, and most pictures were taken between autumn 1990 and June last year. This book is the impressive debut of two former school friends who, both only 24, are the directors of Aerial Images Ltd of Reading. They are now spreading their wings – or rather their revolving blades – over other parts of Britain and the world.

For help with my text I am grateful to several local librarians, but more especially to Denise Silvester-Carr who, as a writer of books on London, brought her extensive knowledge to solve problems. An indefatigable topographer, she spent hours tracing roads from maps and, having identified elusive places, assisted me in putting them into their modern and historical contexts.

FELIX BARKER
LINDSEY HOUSE, BLACKHEATH
1992

The camera, above Marylebone, looks east to capture an autumn dawn. A pale yellow sun is reflected in clouds that lie above a thin blanket of smog over distant Docklands. The Telecom tower (in the foreground) and high buildings, flecked with sunshine, in Euston Road (to the left) are easily discernible, and the stepped white tower of the Senate House of the University of London (right) can also be seen emerging wraith-like from fading darkness.

WHITEHALL AND ST JAMES'S

Government buildings in Whitehall (*left*) are so close to St James's Park that civil servants have only a short distance to walk for lunchtime strolls by the lake, seen here at Duck Island near Horse Guards Parade. This trim royal park, once part of Henry VIII's hunting grounds, was laid out in the reign of Charles II and lies south of the double rows of plane trees on the Mall (*above*), the royal processional route from Buckingham Palace.

Houses with royal associations are to be expected, and a number of them overlook the park. The first group (on the left, *above*, and on the right, *opposite*) is Carlton House Terrace. Seen more impressively from the front (page 123), these stucco houses were built by John Nash on the site of the Prince Regent's palace when it was pulled down in 1827. Marlborough House, in recent years the Commonwealth Secretariat, is the H-shaped red brick building, further along the Mall (*above*). Shortly after their marriage in 1863, the Prince and Princess of Wales (Edward VII and Queen Alexandra) made it their home and much to the annoyance of the Prince's mother, Queen Victoria, began to entertain all fashionable London. To be a member of the 'Marlborough House set' meant one had arrived socially. St James's Palace, where the present Prince of Wales has his office, and Clarence House, the home of Queen Elizabeth the Queen Mother, are barely visible among the trees, but the upper floors and mellow Bath stone of Lancaster House stand out. This is now used as a banqueting house and conference centre.

The square white building catching the sun in the foreground (bottom left) is the Athenaeum, the learned gentlemen's club designed by Decimus Burton in 1828 to complement Nash's nearby buidings. The clump of trees (centre) are in St James's Square, one of the first large building developments undertaken west of the City in the late 17th century, when the Court moved to St James's Palace.

BLOOMSBURY AND WATERLOO STATION

Left The twinkling lights of Bloomsbury and beyond, seen from the top of the Telecom tower, look most attractive at night. This is the area made famous by Virginia Woolf and the Blooms-bury Group. It would be nice to imagine that their successors – students, artists and aspiring writers – were burning midnight oil and carrying on the Bohemian tradition. Bloomsbury was once a fashionable residential area. The streets and squares between High Holborn and Euston Road were developed late in the 17th century, and the houses have mostly been converted into offices, small hotels or halls of residence for university students.

The buildings in the foreground are shops along Tottenham Court Road, the largest of which, Heal's, is the famous long-established bed and furniture store. Once a family business highly regarded for simplicity of design, it was run for many years by Sir Ambrose Heal.

Dominating the aerial view is the elaborately modelled white Portland stone tower of London University's Senate House, which Charles Holden designed in what has been called his 'late stripped-classical' style. As it only peeps above the rest of the building, it is hard to appreciate the size of the copper dome on the British Museum. Sydney Smirke, whose elder brother Robert had been responsible for the museum buildings, designed the circular Reading Room and gave it the splendid dome.

Above Through Waterloo Station, opened in 1846, thousands of passengers are confronted daily with the unprepossessing streets of workaday Southwark.

Close to the station is the famous Old Vic Theatre. Its cream façade on the tersely named Cut can just be glimpsed to the left of the classical columns of a building in the Waterloo Road. Part of Shell Centre, one of the largest office blocks in Europe, is in the bottom left corner.

Soot from factory chimneys once covered the Victorian city in a gloomy pall, and fog was seized on by Hollywood filmmakers to epitomise London. Although steam trains, belching industrial chimneys and coal fires have largely disappeared, with the Clean Air Act forbidding certain fuels, another form of pollution now threatens the environment. Fumes from cars and the damage done to the sun's protective layers produce the 'inversion' seen lying over Docklands (*above*). A line of clear warm air several hundred feet above the East End presses down on the polluted smog over the Isle of Dogs and prevents fog, smoke and haze from clearing.

Strong sunlight casts a shining path across the City at dawn (*right*). The faint outline of Canary Wharf, with cranes on the roof, can be seen in the distance. The National Westminster tower, on the right, and other tall buildings emerge at this dawn stand-to of an army of silhouettes.

RICHMOND AND PUTNEY

Left In a 35-mile camera flight from Richmond to the new bridge at Dartford (page 33), the Thames first passes under the graceful arches of Richmond Bridge and curves north towards Kew. Opposite the stepped terrace of the controversial neo-Georgian re-development (page 145) are two aits, or eyots, an old English word for what were probably once osier islands. Remains of Richmond Palace, a favourite summer home of the Tudor sovereigns, lie hidden among the trees just before the next bridge which is for the railway. Traffic flows across Twickenham Bridge, beyond which are the flat fields of the Old Deer Park, once part of the palace grounds. The park follows the river as it turns towards central London.

Right On this stretch of river from Putney to Barnes the annual University Boat Race was rowed upstream for the first time over 150 years ago. This was before the building of the slender railway crossing and Sir Joseph Bazalgette's five-span Putney Bridge – now the starting point of the race. On the way west to the finish at Mortlake, the Oxford and Cambridge crews pass the bishops of London's former residence, Fulham Palace, in deep shadow on the Middlesex bank (right), before coming to the large reservoirs created on part of the Barn Elms estate of Sir Francis Walsingham, the Tudor statesman.

VAUXHALL TO WANDSWORTH

Left This magnificent S-shaped sweep of the river stretches from Vauxhall Bridge in the foreground to Wandsworth Bridge at the top of the loop in the distance. Next up river is the Victoria Railway Bridge, and beyond that Chelsea, Albert and Battersea bridges.

In Pimlico on the right two large housing estates range back from the river and symbolise two contrasting periods in architecture and living. Nearest is Dolphin Square (1,236 neo-Georgian flats), designed by Gordon Jeeves. It was regarded in 1937 as the last word in snug luxury and carried in its day a faint whiff of upper-class naughtiness. Rising behind Dolphin Square is Churchill Gardens (1,661 flats, the epitome of modern style, 1946-1962), the work of the young Powell and Moya, with blocks of flats varying from six to eleven storeys.

Above From the other direction the view shows Albert Bridge in the foreground, an engineering oddity because it appears to be a suspension bridge but was cantilevered to start with (page 20). One of the most decorative Thames crossings, the bridge links Battersea with Chelsea on the left. The unexpected temple in the trees of Battersea Park, right, is a gilded pagoda built by a sect of Buddhist monks and presented to London in 1985. On the opposite bank, in the grounds of the Royal Hospital (out of view, but see page 118), an obelisk – memorial of the 1849 Sikh war – is a central feature of the annual Chelsea Flower Show.

ALBERT AND VAUXHALL BRIDGES

For almost 1,700 years the only way to cross the Thames on foot between Teddington and the sea was at London Bridge. People had to be ferried from bank to bank. The building of Putney Bridge in 1729, followed by Westminster Bridge in 1750, eased the carriage jams; and soon afterwards bridges were erected at Kew, Richmond, Blackfriars and Battersea. But it was the 19th-century engineers who really started bridge-building in earnest. Between 1811 and 1894 twenty-two new bridges were put up, several – such as London, Blackfriars and Battersea – being replacements for earlier ones.

Albert Bridge (*left*), as the name suggests, belongs to the Victorian era and was opened in 1873. Its cantilever construction was not entirely successful and ten years later Sir Joseph Bazalgette strengthened it with suspension cables. Bazalgette, who designed or altered four other Thames bridges, was also the engineer responsible for the embankments, including Chelsea Embankment – seen here at Cheyne Walk, east of Oakley Street.

The first iron bridge across the Thames was at Vauxhall in 1816, and for a short while it was known as Regent's Bridge. The present bridge (*above*) belongs to this century.

Just visible between the cranes – above the foundations of a new Foreign Office building – at the south-east end of the bridge is a small green area. This is all that remains of the famous Vauxhall Gardens which, in the 18th century, consisted of 20 acres of beautifully landscaped grounds where Handel conducted concerts and elaborate fancy dress balls were held. The gardens closed in 1859. The first Vauxhall Bridge came as a boon. Before it was built it took visitors, including the Prince Regent, three hours by carriage to reach the gardens for the fête celebrating the Duke of Wellington's victory at Vittoria.

PIMLICO AND MILLBANK

The riverside becomes increasingly treeless and more crowded with buildings as the Thames enters central London near Vauxhall Bridge. Upriver, Pimlico is still largely residential, with most of Thomas Cubitt's solid Victorian stucco houses now converted into small hotels or flats. Turn the other way (*above*) and almost every building is commercial. Millbank Tower, shimmering by Lambeth Bridge, is one of the more elegant skyscrapers in London. Just in front of it, the white pedimented building with a small dome is the Tate Gallery (page 82).

Left Between Lambeth and Westminster Bridges, Church and State present a united Gothic front on the west bank, while the Archbishop of Canterbury looks across the river to Westminster Abbey and the Houses of Parliament from his London residence in Lambeth Palace. With a fine Tudor gatehouse, the palace has a large private garden – seen through the trees. As the river turns under Hungerford (Charing Cross railway bridge) and Waterloo Bridges (*below*), the three Barbican towers and the National Westminster tower come into view. On the South Bank, Shell Centre dwarfs both County Hall and the arts centres by Waterloo Bridge.

Right The reflection of the Clock Tower in the river at Westminster Bridge appears to show the hands at six o'clock. Big Ben has announced the time in London since 1859, and it has been world famous since it heralded wartime radio news broadcasts. Not everything went smoothly when the decision was taken to install a clock and bell at the Houses of Parliament. Two years after building finished on the tower in 1854, a great bell, cast in Stockton-on-Tees, was brought up the Thames to Palace Yard where it was suspended on a temporary gantry. But during trials the tone proved unsatisfactory, and the metal cracked. This was melted down for a new bell, which was cast at the Whitechapel Bell Foundry and drawn on a dray by sixteen horses to Westminster through crowd-filled streets.

BLACKFRIARS BRIDGE AND THE SOUTH BANK

Left The mass of 'packing case' office buildings around Queen Victoria Street gives no hint that at ground level the City of London has human interest, thanks to narrow alleys and small courtyards that still meander on lines inherited from medieval builders. Beyond Blackfriars Bridge and the railway bridge – St Paul's Bridge until its name changed also to Blackfriars – are Sea Containers House and King's Reach Tower. The latter appears more clearly earlier in the day looking the other way (*above*), resembling a mellow honeycombed tube. The bridges, going downstream (*above*), are Blackfriars (road and rail), Southwark, Alexandra (the little-known name of Cannon Street railway bridge), London and Tower. Mondial House, likened to a word processor by Prince Charles, is immediately beyond the twin turrets at Cannon Street Station.

TOWER BRIDGE

Most distinctive of all London's bridges, Tower Bridge looks venerable. But despite its medieval appearance this fanciful Gothic structure was built just under a century ago. Horace Jones, the City architect, intended the medieval style to harmonize with the Tower of London, and the chains to give the impression of an ancient drawbridge. The Upper Pool was still commercially in use in the late 19th century, and the raising and lowering of twin bascules in the centre of the road was to allow tall-masted ships to sail through.

A lift in the north-west tower carries visitors to the two high-level walkways from where, 140 feet above the Thames, there are views of the City not dissimilar to those once seen by young sailors in the riggings of their ships. Access to the walkways was stopped in 1909 after they became the haunt of down-and-outs. In 1982 the roofs of the towers were renovated, the sides glazed and the walkways reopened. At the same time a museum was installed in the south tower.

When opened in 1894, Tower Bridge was the last bridge before the Thames reached the sea, a position previously held by London Bridge since about 43 AD. Then in October 1991 the Queen Elizabeth II Bridge at Dartford (page 33) was completed and became the entrance gate to London.

TOWER BRIDGE

Left Large ships today seldom come into the Upper Pool, but HMS *Belfast*, a floating naval museum (*below*), is permanently anchored above Tower Bridge. Built in 1939, she saw service during the Second World War at the Battle of the North Cape in the Arctic Circle in 1943, and was off Normandy for the D-Day landings. She is the largest cruiser (11,000 tons) ever built for the Royal Navy.

Right The *Cutty Sark*, in dry dock at Greenwich, commemorates the golden age of sail. Built in 1869, she is the only fully-rigged survivor of a class that raced home from China to be first at the London tea auctions. A much smaller ship, by the domed entrance to the foot tunnel under the river, *Gypsy Moth IV* is the 54-ft sailing ketch in which, at the age of 66 in 1967, the pioneer aviator-turned-navigator Sir Francis Chichester became the first person to circumnavigate the world single-handed.

Left The free Woolwich Ferry was the first serious attempt to link Kent with Essex. Paddle-steamers were used on the five-minute journey from Woolwich to North Woolwich from 1889 until 1963, when modern ships came into service. Children are said to have been sent regularly on the crossing to recuperate from illnesses: more likely the paddles were the real attraction.

Left Although cargo ships are an infrequent sight since the last docks closed in 1980, a few still land goods. This one is anchored at Lyle Wharf in North Woolwich. Downriver, traffic is a little busier.

Right The Queen Elizabeth II Bridge, opened on 30 October 1991, rises high over the river to link Dartford and Thurrock. With four lanes all carrying south-bound traffic, the Dartford Bridge is 450 metres long (compared to Tower Bridge's 61 metres) and is the largest cable-supported bridge in Europe. The tallest liner can pass under the central span. Built in three years, the £86 million were raised by eight private companies, and tolls should repay the outlay in anything from fourteen to twenty years.

The glories of the river banks fade quickly after the Queen Elizabeth II Bridge, and become bleak and industrial. On the journey east to the North Sea, gasworks, quarries and factories can be discerned as dawn rises over the Essex marshes at West Thurrock in the foreground and, across the river, at Swanscombe in Kent. Twenty winding miles from the estuary and the sea, this is the eerie stretch of river where convict hulks were once moored. The marshlands, cloaked in yellow mist, remain a flat wilderness of ghostly silhouettes.

Historically, this is almost the view of the Essex shore Elizabeth I had when she travelled a short distance further down river to Tilbury Marshes, to rally the troops awaiting the arrival of Philip of Spain's Armada in 1588.

The main dock at Tilbury, which supplanted London, can be seen beyond Fiddler's Reach and North Fleet Hope, where the Thames bends again to Gravesend Reach. The piers, jetties and wharves (some disused now) are reminders of the busy industrial river that for almost 2,000 years was London's main highway.

Opposite Dominating the journey down the Thames, the tower of Canary Wharf on the Isle of Dogs is seen for miles in the distance. Of all London's modern monuments it demands attention from sheer size. Row after row of windows look out from forty-five floors of offices. This cyclopean giant has more single eyes than anyone can conveniently count. Blue protective covering on the left was swept away as the building was completed, leaving the 800-foot monster smooth, changing colour in different lights and more than a little intimidating.

Above Tall buildings are no novelty on the river. This factory, which makes no attempt to disguise its nondescript ugliness, is just one of innumerable industrial buildings which have come to be accepted as necessary features of the Thames as a commercial river.

Right Docklands, with its well-named Enterprise Zone, is proud of its architectural daring, and the Cascades building at the entrance to the West India Docks claims part of its inspiration from the tall ships that once used the basin. The 171-apartment block (designers Campbell, Zogolovitch, Wilkinson and Gough) was completed in 1988 at the height of the property boom when prices of the balconied apartments ranged from £100,000 to £335,000. From the back of the upper floors, residents are able to see another architectural curiosity, the red wood facades of the Scandinavian-style development resting on stilts on the edge of Heron Quays. In his *A Vision of Britain* the Prince of Wales criticises the Cascades as 'aggressive' and 'inappropriately high', and thinks 'the edge of the river should be more sacrosanct'.

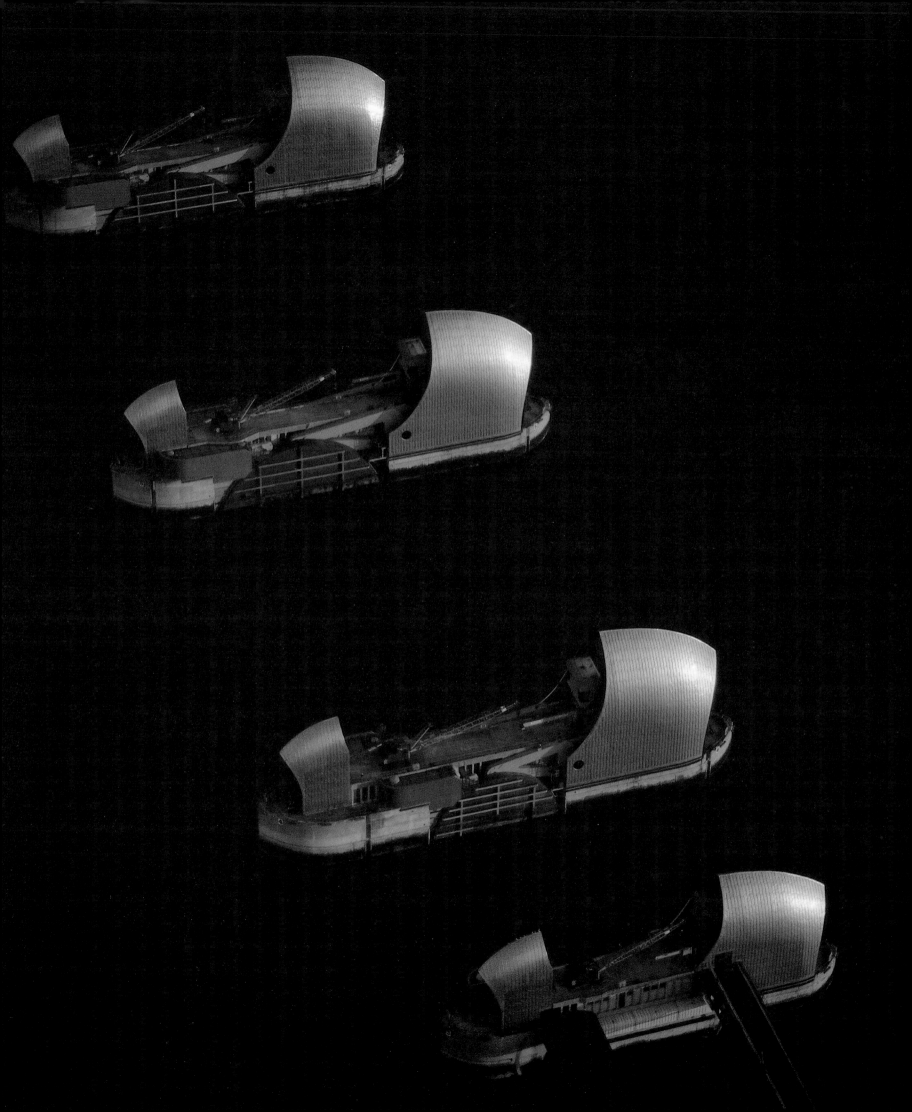

THE THAMES BARRIER

Shimmering metal hoods, resembling the helmets of medieval knights, protect machinery on
the concrete piers that span the Thames at Woolwich. Ten separate steel-plated gates between
the piers can be raised to form a continuous wall to hold back the river and prevent flooding in
London. Normally the massive gates of the Thames Barrier (described as 'the Eighth Wonder
of the World' by the Queen when she opened it in 1983) lie on the river bed, enabling ships to
pass upriver to the docks near Canary Wharf, which can be glimpsed on the skyline *above*.

CANARY WHARF

Above, left Built by a Canadian company, Canary Wharf covers seventy acres and is the largest redevelopment project in the United Kingdom. The name is derived from the Canary Islands, from which wine and fruit were brought, and landed here, before trading in the West India Docks ceased in 1980. The main tower, with forty-five floors of offices, rises to 800 feet, making it the tallest building in Britain and beating its nearest rival, the National Westminster tower in the City (on the skyline), by 180 feet. It is surrounded by thirty other office buildings. To make the potential 60,000 business people feel cossetted there is a shopping mall with boutiques, hairdressers and food hall. A sports centre and fitness gymnasium will keep them toned up.

Above, right As this view shows, the pyramid-shaped roof of the Canary Wharf tower (designed by Cesar Pelli) partly obstructs the view of Greenwich Park, and, from the other direction, the view northwards from the top of the park is spoilt, which annoys residents south of the river. The tower is again condemned by that royal arbiter of architectural taste, the Prince of Wales, who has a low opinion of high-rise buildings and calls it 'monstrous'. As lip-service to early architects, such as Wren, Adam and Nash, their names have been given to the watercourts and squares on the Wharf. The Canadian corporation responsible for the project has also commemorated explorers who opened up North America. Cabot Square can just be seen beyond Wren Landing, which is immediately to the right of the pale yellow building on the edge of Fisherman's Wharf. The overall plan of Canary Wharf (by Skidmore, Owings and Merrill) provided the guidelines and a number of leading international architects were then invited to design the individual buildings.

Right A light to warn aircraft – especially planes approaching London City Airport – winks continuously on the top of the pyramid. From the tower the Essex and Kent banks of the river are clearly visible and the airport's runway can be seen on the long wharf in the Royal Docks

Above, left Expensive yachts and motor launches are today berthed in Chelsea Harbour, a luxurious complex of town houses, apartments, offices, the Conrad Hotel, shopping malls and restaurants designed by Moxley, Jenner & Partners. In the late 19th century this was a basin for barges towed from the Thames along the now-forgotten Kensington Canal to the Grand Union Canal. Built on a rundown site towards the end the 1980s, Chelsea Harbour has a twenty-storey tower, the Belvedere, which has one apartment only on each floor, making these homes among the most expensive in London.

Left The Brunswick Centre's modern-looking terraced apartments, designed at the end of the 1960s (by Patrick Hodgkinson), are a long way from the traditional squares and terraces of Georgian houses which typified Bloomsbury until the Second World War.

Above The fluted semi-circular roof of Frobisher Crescent is one of the main exterior parts of the Barbican Centre. Under it are two of the Centre's three cinemas, rooms for seminars, offices and the City of London Business School. The harsh exterior of the large arts centre, conceived in the 1960s (Chamberlin, Powell and Bon), and finally opened in 1982, has some compensation in the interior, especially the large theatre and concert hall. Several storeys above ground level, the open space in front of the crescent is used for displays of sculpture and, occasionally in the summer, for open-air concerts.

Left The three apartment-block towers at the Barbican are named Cromwell, Shakespeare and Lauderdale (foreground), after famous men associated with the area. Oliver Cromwell was married in nearby St Giles Cripplegate; William Shakespeare wrote *Othello* while lodging in a house now lost in modern London Wall; and Lauderdale is a reminder of John Maitland, first Earl of Lauderdale, who had a house by Aldersgate in the reign of Charles I.

Above The National Westminster Tower in Bishopsgate (Richard Seifert) which until Canary Wharf was completed had a ten-year reign as the country's tallest building.

Above The views overlooking Hyde Park from the roof restaurant at the Hilton Hotel in Park Lane are particularly fine, but when the hotel was built in the early 1960s the kind of people who are always determined to find fault with anything new declared that the gardens of Buckingham Palace were overlooked. The Queen's privacy might be invaded by diners armed with telescopes and binoculars! The trees visible in the top right corner are not however in the Palace grounds but in Green Park, and those fringing the bottom of the view are in Hyde Park.

Left As if determined to defy tradition and its 17th-century background, Lloyd's of London went daringly modern when it decided in 1979 to build new headquarters in Leadenhall Street. Shining pipes containing electricity, heating and other services run along the exterior of the revolutionary building. Openly flaunting what most buildings try to hide, the external cleaning equipment – resembling blue dragonflies – perches on the outside around the Crystal Palace-style central gallery. Richard Rogers's design for the insurance market is a far cry from the coffee house in which Edward Lloyd began trading 300 years ago, but the Adam Room (where the Council of Lloyd's meets) from an earlier building was incorporated into the new structure – as was the Lutine Bell, rung to announce important news. Brilliant outside lighting, which appears to change colour, causes fanciful transformations at night.

TELECOM TOWER

It is hard to keep pace with 'Telecom'. A dancing Pan-like logo – symbolising the 'spirit of communications' – and the letters 'BT' are due to replace the word 'Telecom' early in 1992 on the tower near Tottenham Court Road. Originally erected for the Post Office and opened in 1965, the 620-foot slimline tower has a number of circular discs beneath the once-revolving restaurant. Mystifying to the uninitiated, these microwave dishes beam telecommunications signals to similar directly aligned discs. The viewing platform and restaurant were closed to the public for security reasons in 1975.

Left The West India Docks, which opened in 1802, were the first and the finest of the enclosed 19th-century docks. Looking down at them now from the air, the great protective walls and the five-storey warehouses which stretched in a continuous line for three-quarters of a mile can only be imagined. Gone amid new buildings is the heady aroma of sugar and rum landed on the quays. The main tower of the new development stands on the site of a banana warehouse, and the resemblance between some buildings and the World Financial Center at Battery Park City in New York is probably because the same architect (Cesar Pelli) worked on both schemes. At the time of its construction, a brilliant blue protective covering on the tower was mystifying and caused some concern – was the building to be two-coloured? – until it was re-moved to reveal the gleaming stainless steel cladding.

Above Nature abhors a vacuum and people are suspicious if a huge new building is left empty for years – as was Centre Point, the much-discussed office block where Oxford Street and Charing Cross Road meet. Designed in the mid-1960s (Richard Seifert and Partners) for a reclusive property developer, the long-untenanted Centre Point aroused much speculation. Was a waiting game a commercial gambit? Occupied, it still looks grandiose but has some redeeming grace.

Above Wapping has lost its evil reputation and been given a new lease of life. Trendy town houses now surround the docks where tobacco, brandy, wine and rice were landed in the last century. Victorian warehouses have been converted into apartments and studios; clean new industries have opened; and a fresh generation of professional people have come to live in the area. The dark barrel roofs (centre) cover the shops and restaurants which have been attractively sited in the restored vaulted warehouses of Tobacco Dock.

When the London Docks closed in 1969 an air of sad neglect pervaded the twisting streets and alleys until regeneration, started in the 1980s, brought a transformation to this bombed and rundown district. Churches such as Nicholas Hawksmoor's St George-in-the-East (in the centre, to the right), much neglected for a century, have found a new role to play.

Right In the early 19th century, the opening of the London Docks and the population expansion came at the same time as the railways. Houses for former City residents started to be built on fields south of the river, especially alongside London's first railway – an almost straight line for most of the way from London Bridge to Greenwich. The line seen here, which opened in 1836, appears to cut through rows of houses, but was built when there were open fields.

The large grey tower block (on the right) is a modern addition to Guy's Hospital. The early Georgian hospital – founded by Thomas Guy in 1721 to alleviate overcrowding at nearby St Thomas's Hospital – lies in front of the eleven-storey tower. On the other side of the forecourt two later Georgian wings are set around quadrangles.

Southwark Cathedral (foreground) is one of the few Gothic churches in London. Near the recently excavated Rose and Globe theatres, the church has close associations with Shakespeare (whose younger brother Edmund was buried here) and other Elizabethan playwrights.

MANSION HOUSE AND THE STOCK EXCHANGE

In these two views, the Palladian portico and pediment of the Mansion House look slightly incongruous next to the City's modern buildings, but would be rather less so if more could be seen of the classical façade of the Royal Exchange (as it is on page 58). Here the columned portico is not in the camera's view, and only the baroque steeple on the east end (with the white roof) is visible. The Mansion House (by George Dance the Elder) has been the official residence of the Lord Mayor of London since 1752. The tower (right) is the Stock Exchange.

Overleaf The City, looking east down the Thames, from above St Paul's. St Mary-le-Bow in Cheapside is in the foreground.

Left At the hub of the City, with streets radiating from it, the Royal Exchange lies between the Mansion House and the Bank of England. The present Exchange, with a great Corinthian portico (by Sir William Tite), replaced the late 17th-century Exchange burnt down in 1838. The first, earlier, place of exchange had been the idea of Sir Thomas Gresham. Impressed by bourses on the Continent, he built premises which were let to merchants and traders – rather like a modern shopping mall. In 1570 it was opened by Queen Elizabeth I. Over 400 years later the second Queen Elizabeth opened the rebuilt present Exchange, which was altered internally in 1991 to give it an extra floor under a new roof.

To the left of the Exchange stands the Bank of England. The Bank had been trading for 40 years when in 1734 it decided to move close to the Royal Exchange. Gone now is Christopher Wren's first City church – St Christopher le Stocks – demolished when the bank was enlarged in 1781. But the churchyard was left an open space and this was retained during two subsequent rebuildings. The small garden at the base of the large rectangular well is on the site, with a lawn and flowerbeds overlooked by the governor and directors when they meet in the Court Room. This fine room was incorporated into Sir John Soane's late 18th-century bank, and Herbert Baker also kept it intact when he entirely rebuilt all the offices inside Soane's strong, formidable surrounding walls.

Above In the centre of this view – but not as tall as the National Westminster Tower – is Lloyd's, which with this cluster of buildings symbolises the invisible earnings that are the City's life blood. Insurance companies, commodity markets, exchanges and international banks help to maintain London's position among the world's three leading financial centres. To justify innovations the City always maintains that business calls for modern facilities, and that is why the oldest district of London is determined to be the most modern architecturally.

THE EAST END

The East End of London is apt to be ignored or taken for granted by guide books, but these two views give the area the perspective it deserves. It needs an aerial photograph to show how the Mile End Road (*right*) forms the entry from Essex and the eastern counties into Whitechapel, Aldgate and so into the heart of the City. The view *above* has the London Hospital – the Royal London Hospital since it was given a royal charter to mark its 250th anniversary in 1990 – in Whitechapel at its centre. The camera picks out the helicopter pad for emergencies, on a modern extension to the west of the main building in the Whitechapel Road. At one time it was the finest hospital in the capital and the first to have a medical school. This was set up by Sir William Blizard, a founder of the Royal College of Surgeons, at the end of the 18th century.

Besides famous physicians and surgeons, the hospital has had famous patients, such as John Merrick, the deformed 'Elephant Man', given accommodation here for many years. It even has a gruesome connection with Jack the Ripper, whose first victim, Mary Anne Nicholls, was killed on the waste land (at the top left hand corner of the view) in Durward Street. A piece of kidney brought to the hospital in 1888 for the resident pathologist to examine was deduced to have come from the dismembered body of Catherine Eddowes, the Ripper's fourth victim. The visible stretch of the Mile End Road (*right*) runs from Grove Road and Regent's Canal to Whitechapel Road and the hospital in the distance. The mile that gives the road its name lies between these points. In the right hand foreground is Queen Mary's College, the science and engineering department of London University. Next to it is the Queen's Hall of the People's Palace. This is the 1930s' replacement of the hall opened by Queen Victoria in 1887 to provide entertainment for working people in the district.

MARBLE ARCH AND OXFORD STREET

Marble Arch, isolated among trees at the west end of Oxford Street, was placed at the Cumberland Gate entrance to Hyde Park in 1850. The triumphal arch, resembling the Arch of Constantine in Rome, was originally at the entrance to the forecourt of Buckingham Palace. When the east front of the palace was built, the arch had to be removed. John Nash wanted to put Sir Francis Chantry's statue of George IV on top, but this equestrian sculpture went instead to Trafalgar Square.

On its island position, with traffic constantly roaring by, the arch is seldom used and only privileged people are permitted to drive through the central gate. They include members of the royal family and the King's Troop of the Royal Horse Artillery, who ride through hauling gun carriages to fire the salute on certain royal birthdays and important state occasions.

A small bronze triangle set in the ground west of the Marble Arch commemorates the most gruesome spot in London – the triple tree at Tyburn. This was the site of the gallows on which thousands were hanged between 1196 and 1783. The unfortunate men and women, whose crimes were often petty offences, were driven in carts through crowds from Newgate – the present Old Bailey – along Oxford Street (*right*). Today Oxford Street is thronged with a very different crowd. Instead of a macabre spectacle, they come to see the shops. Among the sprawl of light-coloured buildings, it is just possible to identify the best known store in the street – Selfridges (centre, between Orchard Street, which leads to Portman Square with trees, and Duke Street, which leads to the smaller Manchester Square). It would have stood out more conspicuously had its founder, Gordon Selfridge, succeeded in a capricious idea of having a monumental tower on top. This was planned at the end of the First World War but the project was abandoned when it was calculated that the weight would crush the shop.

HYDE PARK CORNER

A bird's view (*left*) of Hyde Park Corner reveals a trivial feature in the grounds of Buckingham Palace – a hard tennis court. Of more consequence are Constitution Arch, Apsley House, the new Lanesborough Hotel (on the left) and the statue of Achilles in Hyde Park. Constitution Arch (formerly called the Wellington Arch) was designed in 1825 by Decimus Burton and originally stood in line with the Ionic screen that was the grand entrance to the park from Buckingham Palace. Burton stipulated that a quadriga should be placed on top of the arch, but when moved it was surmounted by an equestrian statue of the Duke of Wellington. This so annoyed the architect that for many years he kept a clause in his will leaving £2,000 to remove the 'Iron Duke'. Two years after his death in 1881 the authorities acceded to his wishes at the instigation, it is said, of Queen Victoria – because she objected to driving under a well-endowed stallion. The statue was taken to Aldershot and Sir Joseph Edgar Boehm's smaller figure of the Duke on his horse Copenhagen went up in 1888 opposite Apsley House. The present Peace Quadriga is a memorial to Edward VII.

Apsley House – at one time known as No 1 London – was built by Robert Adam for Henry Bathurst, Baron Apsley. The house was purchased by the Marquess of Wellesley in 1805. He, in his turn, resold it to his brother, the 1st Duke of Wellington. Although the Iron Duke's descendant – the 8th Duke – maintains an apartment in the house, it is now a museum housing paintings and the spoils of the Iron Duke's victories.

The most recent building at Hyde Park Corner is the Lanesborough Hotel, which has been built behind the preserved façade of St George's Hospital, opened in 1733 near the turnpike at the main entrance to London from the west. The hotel takes its name from James Lane, 2nd Viscount Lanesborough, the owner of the house which became St George's.

PICCADILLY CIRCUS AND OXFORD CIRCUS

The original names of Piccadilly Circus (*above*) and Oxford Circus (*right*) were fortunately changed in the 19th century. Otherwise it would be very confusing. Previously both circuses were called Regent Circus. They were named after the Prince Regent who, when John Nash was planning the thoroughfare from Carlton House to Regent's Park, insisted that something should be done 'to prevent the sensation of crossing Piccadilly'. Nash eliminated conventional crossroads by placing curved buildings on each corner. The junction at Oxford Street has more or less kept its circular shape, but Piccadilly Circus has altered a great deal. It became badly distorted when Shaftesbury Avenue was cut into the Circus in 1886, and buildings were demolished to make room for more modern replacements. The Regency quadrants round Oxford Circus were also entirely rebuilt between 1913 and 1928.

In recent years Piccadilly Circus, once nicknamed the Hub of the British Empire, appears to have lost lustre. This coincides with the decision to re-orientate the statue of Eros. No longer on an island in the middle of the road, this memorial to the philanthropic Earl of Shaftesbury is now accessible to all on a pavement from the south. The strange name 'Piccadilly' is thought to derive from the 'pickadills' or shirt frills sold at Piccadilly House by Robert Baker early in the 17th century. The house was at the south end of Windmill Street, seen (*above*) in the foreground on the east side of the triangular roof of the London Pavilion.

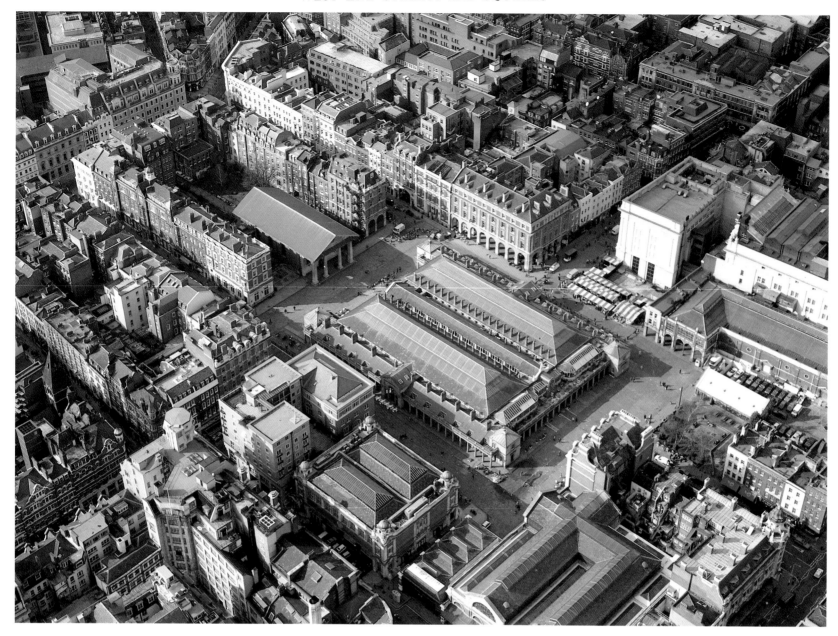

Above St Paul's, Covent Garden, looks like a fine barn from the air. This is as it should be. Inigo Jones's patron, Francis Russell, the 4th Earl of Bedford, wasn't prepared to spend money on a church which produced little revenue. When he asked for something simple – 'not much better than a barn' – Jones's reply was that it would be 'the handsomest barn in Europe'. The central market buildings, put up in the piazza in 1830, yielded a large income for the Russells, but by the time trading in fruit and vegetables ceased in 1974 the land was no longer owned by the Bedford Estates. The 9th Duke of Bedford had sold out in 1918. The renaissance of Covent Garden has come with the fashionable redevelopment of the market.

Right, top Leicester Square means entertainment. Large cinemas, the five-star Hampshire Hotel and restaurants flank three sides. The aerial camera catches the central gardens at a time in 1991 when a crane is part of excavation work to create an underground power station. The white dome is over part of the modern Swiss Centre, but the circular grey roof with a domed skylight is a reminder of a much earlier form of entertainment. The Church of Notre Dame de France was converted from a rotunda built in 1793 to accommodate Robert Barker's Panorama. For almost three-quarters of a century the Panorama gave audiences the illusion of being surrounded by views and dramatic events, much as the Leicester Square cinemas have done for the last fifty years.

Right, bottom In Cambridge Circus, the curved red brick and terracotta building with domed turrets (centre) is the Palace Theatre, Shaftesbury Avenue. Built as the home of English opera for Richard D'Oyly Carte, it later became a variety theatre; and here the Russian ballerina Pavlova made her first public London appearance in 1910. Andrew Lloyd Webber, whose show *Jesus Christ Superstar*, ran at the Palace for eight years, now owns the theatre.

CHINATOWN, SHAFTESBURY AVENUE AND TRAFALGAR SQUARE

Left More than slightly self-conscious, like an amateur actor playing Dr Fu Manchu, London's Chinatown lies between Shaftesbury Avenue and Lisle Street. Pagoda-shaped arches can be seen at either end of Gerrard Street, with barriers to preserve a pedestrian precinct. Telephone boxes and street furniture are decorated in oriental style, and about all that is lacking is a property rickshaw. Even the street signs are bi-lingual.

Right Shaftesbury Avenue, seen here running from Cambridge Circus up the left side of the picture, was laid out in 1886 and given the name of the 7th Earl of Shaftesbury, whose philanthropy brought relief to many poor people who lived in slums swept away by the new street. Cosmopolitan Soho lies mainly to the right of the street which, with five theatres, is the centre of West End theatreland. The clock tower in the distance, which has a small garden on the far side, is all that survives of St Anne's, Soho, a church bombed during the Second World War.

Opposite Trafalgar Square after a snowfall. The massive triumphal arch at the end of the Mall (top right) is Admiralty Arch; and in the square, Canada House, on the right, faces South Africa House (by Sir Herbert Baker). The block curving into the Strand is Grand Buildings, modern shops and offices with decorative carved masonry where a Victorian hotel once stood.

TRAFALGAR SQUARE

Trafalgar Square was described as 'the finest site in Europe' by Sir Robert Peel, the Victorian Prime Minister – a chauvinistic exaggeration, however much Londoners might like to agree. Certainly it is the largest public square in the city, and was planned by John Nash as part of his 'Grand Improvements'. When Nash died in 1835 only the demolition of the Royal Mews and narrow streets around St Martin-in-the-Fields (*right*, top left) had taken place, though work had begun on the National Gallery (*above*, top right). Laying out the square fell to Sir Charles Barry, who levelled the sloping central area and created a raised terrace in front of the gallery. The decision to name it after the naval battle was not immediate, and there was no thought of putting up a statue to Nelson until the suggestion appeared in a letter to *The Times* in 1837. Six years after that the statue was placed on top of a 170-foot Corinthian column.

The statue of Charles I on the triangular island faces Whitehall towards the site of his execution. A plaque at the base pinpoints the generally accepted centre of London, from which mileages are reckoned. This was the site of the final cross put up by Edward I to mark the resting places of his wife's funeral procession to Westminster Abbey in 1291. Long after it was destroyed in 1647, a Victorian replacement of Eleanor's Cross went up outside Charing Cross Station (*right,* top right).

Left Government buildings in Whitehall, stately verging on the ponderous, are seen here parallel with the Embankment which is in the foreground. Richmond Terrace, in the street of the same name, faces the green-roofed Ministry of Defence. Downing Street, on the far side of Whitehall, runs west towards St James's Park, with the Foreign and Commonwealth Offices to the south and the garden wall of No 10 is on the edge of Horse Guards Parade.

Whitehall today is a wide, tree-lined street, totally unlike its predecessor which developed over the centuries after Henry VIII seized York House from Cardinal Wolsey. Henry's rambling Palace of Whitehall was altered by the Stuart kings, who added the Privy Gardens and outbuildings where the Ministry of Defence now stands. The palace was largely destroyed by fire in 1698.

The Cenotaph, the national memorial to the dead of two World Wars, is in the centre of the road. This simple monument to those with no known grave was erected in 1919 and helped to make the designer, Sir Edwin Lutyens, the most famous British architect of his day.

Above As modern Whitehall was taking shape, squares and terraces with large stuccoed houses were being built on meadows west and south of Buckingham Palace. Belgravia, London's most fashionable district after Mayfair, was coming into being. Like Mayfair, Belgravia is part of the Duke of Westminster's estate and was created with extraordinary flair between 1825 and 1855 by the great 19th-century developer Thomas Cubitt. He leased the land from the Duke's ancestor, the 2nd Earl Grosvenor, and Eaton Square had a dignity and charm which quickly made it fashionable. The square, which takes its name from Eaton, the Grosvenor family's estate in Cheshire, is divided by the King's Road, seen here running north-east between snow-covered gardens towards St Peter's, Eaton Square (top left). Only by the wildest definition can it be called a square. Eaton Oblong should really be its name.

SLOANE SQUARE AND CADOGAN PLACE

Large areas of London are in the hands of private owners – the Grosvenors, Russells, Portmans – and in Chelsea the land between Knightsbridge and the river belongs to Earl Cadogan. The Cadogan name and that of Sloane are everywhere. It began in 1771 when Elizabeth Sloane, a rich heiress, married the 2nd Earl Cadogan, an alliance which gave birth to the Cadogan Estate. She had inherited most of the extensive land from her father, Sir Hans Sloane, the Court physician and antiquary. As soon as he had control of the land, Lord Cadogan leased 100 acres to Henry Holland, who laid out Cadogan Place (*right*) and Sloane Square (*above*), linking them when he subsequently developed Sloane Street.

Above Sloane Square has two notable buildings: one – on the corner of the square and by the King's Road (foreground, left) – is Peter Jones, hailed in 1936 as a fine, pioneering example of 'curtain-wall' design (by W. Crabtree), and famous for elegant furniture and fabrics. The other is the Royal Court Theatre, which from the early days of Shaw and Granville-Barker to Osborne and George Devine has held a special place in theatrical history. Facing the square on the east side, the Royal Court turns its angry back on prosperous Eaton Square.

   Two-towered Holy Trinity church, at the Sloane Square end of Sloane Street ('the outstanding example of the Arts and Crafts Movement', according to Sir Nikolaus Pevsner), has a fine Sir Edward Burne-Jones window by William Morris.

Right Going north towards Knightsbridge, Sloane Street is crossed by Pont Street. The snow-covered grass to the right in front of the Hyatt Carlton Tower Hotel is Cadogan Place. The elaborately decorated gabled red brick and terracotta houses in the street to the left are in a style described as 'Pont Street Dutch' by the architectural satirist Osbert Lancaster.

MUSEUMLAND

Left Albertopolis was the ironical, but at the same time admiring, name given by the Victorians to an area of Kensington, seen here, which was planned by the Prince Consort as a centre for the arts and sciences. 'Museumland' was an even more apt name. Profits from the 1851 Great Exhibition in Hyde Park were used to purchase eighty-seven acres for institutions which remain astonishing in their variety. The Royal College of Art, Royal College of Needlework, Royal College of Music and Royal College of Organists are all near the Royal Albert Hall (page 80), towards the top of the view. To this diversity were added museums which have recently broadened their appeal to become entertaining as well as enlightening.

The Natural History Museum, in the middle foreground, by Alfred Waterhouse, may be a flamboyant Romanesque building but it has modern laboratories for the latest scientific research. The museum was opened in 1881 with collections relating to zoology, entomology, palaeontology and mineralogy. Now, exhibitions explain such modern hazards as the greenhouse effect and the destruction of the rain forests.

Behind the Natural History Museum, the Geological Museum illustrates the story of the earth, while the Science Museum, next door, demonstrates scientific advances. The 300-foot Queen's Tower is all that remains of the Imperial Institute, forerunner of the Commonwealth Institute.

Above The vast Victoria and Albert Museum, designed by Francis Fowke, is devoted to the art and design of all manner of splendid objects – porcelain, jewellery, prints or furniture – with period rooms reflecting Gothic, Renaissance and 18th-century rococo tastes. Facing it, across the road, is the London headquarters of the Ismailia Council (designed by Sir Hugh Casson).

THE ROYAL ALBERT HALL

This round building would immediately declare its identity as the Albert Hall if the Albert Memorial across Kensington Road could be properly seen. An amphitheatre capable of holding an audience of over 8,000 for concerts and sporting events, the Albert Hall was one of the vast buildings in Museumland inspired by Henry Cole, and designed by Francis Fowke. Cole suggested it would be a suitable memorial to the Prince Consort, to whom he had been so indefatigable an administrator. Four years before the 'Hall of Arts and Sciences' opened in 1871, Queen Victoria decided it should have the prefix 'Royal Albert'. Cole financed the large circular building by selling 1,300 seats on 999-year leases. This entitled the owners to free admission to performances, a dynastic arrangement still partly surviving. The Commissioners of the Great Exhibition contributed £50,000 and rented the land for one shilling a year – an amount still payable to their successors.

The Albert Memorial in Kensington Gardens is seen (*right*), in what appears to be a giant sentry box. This hides a larger-than-life statue of the seated Prince Consort, who is being cleaned, repaired, and generally spruced up. This was sculpted after his death. Some may prefer the 1858 large bronze statue at the back of the Albert Hall, which shows the Prince in his Garter robes, but they may be perplexed by what on close examination appear to be Robin Hood boots.

THE TATE GALLERY

On the river near Vauxhall Bridge, the Tate Gallery holds the national collection of modern paintings. It opened in 1897 and owes its existence to a sugar refiner, Sir Henry Tate. Tate donated his own collection of Victorian paintings, and since then the Duveen family of art dealers and, most recently, Charles Clore, another businessman, have financed extensions. The Clore Gallery (designed by James Stirling) was opened in 1987 for an incomparable collection of paintings by Turner. This is the yellow building to the right of the classical portico.

THE QUEEN'S HOUSE AND ROYAL NAVAL COLLEGE, GREENWICH

Four miles below London Bridge the dispiriting commercial river bursts into 'one of the sublime sights of English architecture', as it was described by Professor Sir Charles Reilly. The buildings on the river at Greenwich, left and above, are a visual symphony orchestrated by the most celebrated designers of the 17th and 18th centuries, among them Inigo Jones, John Webb, Sir Christopher Wren, Nicholas Hawksmoor, Sir John Vanbrugh and James 'Athenian' Stuart. Intended as a new palace for Charles II, they became instead Greenwich Hospital, a naval home for retired seamen run on the same lines as the Royal Hospital, Chelsea (page 118).

Two centuries before the palatial classical buildings went up, this was the Palace of Placentia, a Tudor retreat favoured by Henry VIII and Elizabeth I, both of whom were born here.

Separate – almost disdainfully so – is the Queen's House (at the top of the picture, *left*) built for Anne of Denmark, James I's Queen, by Inigo Jones as a pleasure pavilion. This incomparable little house, completed in 1635 for Henrietta Maria, survived the depredation of Placentia during the Civil War. After the Restoration the widowed Henrietta Maria returned to her little 'house of delights', and Inigo Jones's pupil, John Webb, increased the accommodation for the Dowager Queen. One of Wren's few disastrous plans – to pull down this little gem and replace it by a domed building – was fortunately frustrated by William III's wife, Queen Mary.

With an appropriately classical look, the colonnades connecting the Queen's House to the wings of what became the Royal Naval Asylum were erected in 1809. This 'asylum' was a school for boys which moved in 1933, the year before the present National Maritime Museum was founded.

THE ROYAL NAVAL COLLEGE

A closer, more detailed look at the Greenwich buildings shows the palace on the site of Placentia which Charles II wanted to rival Louis XIV's palace at Versailles. Because of the Dutch wars he was unable to find the money, and John Webb had to abandon the King Charles block, completed latterly (bottom right). It was Queen Mary who decided to finish the building as a hospital for veteran sailors. Greenwich Hospital became 'the darling object of her life'. She resolutely preserved the Queen's House with the fine central river view which Wren would have destroyed. The Queen Anne block (left, foreground) was built to match the Charles II wing (right foreground), and the colonnaded ranges behind them, topped by Wren's domes, were finished by Hawksmoor and Vanbrugh, whose colleague Sir James Thornhill decorated the Painted Hall in the King William block (middle right).

Greenwich Hospital ceased to be a home for naval pensioners in 1869, by which time the veterans of Trafalgar and the Napoleonic Wars were dying off. Five years later it became the Royal Naval College, and today it is a staff college of diminishing size for officers of the defence forces.

ST PAUL'S CATHEDRAL

Impervious to the height of buildings that threaten to hem it in, St Paul's manages to remain London's greatest landmark and most dramatic silhouette. Christopher Wren saw to that. To the famous inscription about him in the Crypt ('If you would see his monument look around you') can now be added 'Look *down* on it'. When we do, a secret is revealed. St Paul's, completed in 1709 when Wren was seventy-six, possesses an architectural illusion. An explanation on the next page becomes clear after a study of the pictures here.

Above Aerial photography now reveals the secret known to comparatively few people. Quite simply, the cathedral has false walls. To give St Paul's classical grandeur, Wren built an outer screen all round the main walls. This screen looks impressive from the outside, and cunningly disguises the fact that the nave is supported by buttresses like a Gothic building. The upper windows have no glass; they don't need any because they do not give on to the inside of the cathedral: simply on to open space. Wren has been criticised for this architectural deception but his device has to be admired for its ingenuity. So, too, has his treatment of the dome – the last part of St Paul's to be built and the ultimate expression of Wren's sense of the spectacular. But here again, what can be seen from the outside is very different inside. The dome covers a brick cone supporting the lantern and cross, and below that is a smaller dome low enough for James Thornhill's murals to be appreciated from the ground. As a final piece of architectural conjuring, Wren secured the base of the dome from splaying by encircling it in iron chains.

Right Westminster Abbey is the most impressive Gothic church in London and has the longest verifiable history. Technically it is not a cathedral or a parish church. It is a 'royal peculiar', and as such the Dean and Chapter are answerable only to the sovereign. Once a Benedictine monastery, the Collegiate Church of St Peter was rebuilt by Edward the Confessor and consecrated in 1065.

   Here again the view from the air shows something not appreciated from the ground. There is a truncated central tower cut off a few feet about the ridge of the roof. This can only mean that early builders intended an impressive central tower or spire never fulfilled. When he supervised the restoration of the Abbey in 1698, Wren had the idea of adding this missing feature. So in the 19th century did Charles Barry, the designer of the Houses of Parliament. But neither plan came about.

WESTMINSTER CATHEDRAL AND THE LONDON MOSQUE

Above With the anti-Catholic prejudices that lingered on through the 19th century, it was hardly surprising that Westminster Cathedral with its towering campanile, begun in 1894, was initially received with criticism and ridicule. A 'streaky bacon coloured caricature of an electric light station' was how one satirist described the contrasting bands of red brick and Portland stone that rose 284 feet above Victoria. The design (by John Francis Bentley) was loosely based on the Duomo in Siena.

Now, very much a part of the London scene, the premier church of England's Roman Catholics is accepted, even admired. Derision might well be thought misplaced in a country where Catholic worship is outstripping Protestant. Architecturally the cathedral has an alien look, but serves as a reminder that before the Reformation almost all places of worship belonged to the Catholic Church. Westminster Cathedral, consecrated in 1903, also stands as a memorial to Cardinal Wiseman, the first Archbishop of Westminster, and was built on the site of the demolished Tothill Fields Prison.

Right Considerably more alien to London, despite the growing Asian population, is the golden dome and Arabian-looking minaret on the mosque (by Sir Frederick Gibberd) in Regent's Park. Though it was completed only thirteen years ago, it still startles in this London environment. Those who find the architecture rather too exotic for their tastes can perhaps take comfort from the mosque's resemblance to the Royal Pavilion in Brighton. And are there not also domes of a kind (page 152) on nearby Sussex Place? Responsible as he was for the park's terraces and for the onion domes on the Prince Regent's seaside Indian pavilion, the white building and glittering dome might well have pleased John Nash.

THE TOWER OF LONDON

The Tower of London has no difficulty in maintaining its position as one of the country's main tourist attractions. Nearly three million visitors come from all over the world to relish its gory past. The place where kings and queens, common criminals and traitors have been held captive or executed is box-office. The turnstiles revolve briskly as people pay to see the Crown Jewels and suits of armour.

This view from the south east makes it possible to look over the central White Tower which William the Conqueror ordered 900 years ago as part of his defences to protect London from invaders. Later, walls with flanking towers encircled a moat which was drained in the last century and grassed over.

The only defensive fortification to survive on the river, except Windsor Castle, the Tower once had royal apartments on the upper floor of the White Tower; but few sovereigns chose to live there except at times of disorder. Over nine centuries the fortress has evolved into the present conglomeration of towers, storehouses, chapels and houses. On the river, in the foreground, is Traitors' Gate, through which Elizabeth I was taken when her sister Mary I imprisoned her in the Bell Tower (on the left of the inner wall in the foreground).

The Law Courts in the Strand (*above*) and the Houses of Parliament (*right*) have much in common. Each is an extravagant example of Victorian Gothic architecture, and both owe their existence to a fire in 1834. When the medieval Palace of Westminster – to give the Houses of Parliament their old royal title – was burnt down, the civil law courts which were part of the building were also destroyed. For centuries these had been housed in Westminster Hall or in the huddle of adjoining buildings that the architect Sir Charles Barry described as 'a mere excrescence upon Westminster Hall'. Although the hall, with the deep-pitched roof and lantern to the left of Big Ben (*right, above*), survived the fire and became part of the new Houses of Parliament, Barry was unable to find space for the Law Courts – or the Royal Courts of Justice as they are officially called. The government bought an area of slum land on the Strand, within a lazy lawyer's walk of the Inns of Court, and held a competition for their design.

The Victorians favoured such competitions, which nearly always resulted in acrimonious arguments. Barry and his collaborator, Augustus Welby Pugin, were selected to build the Houses of Parliament and then forced to alter their plans a number of times; the Victoria Tower and Big Ben were on the original drawings but the central spire was an afterthought, a ventilation shaft put up at the insistence of an engineer so that, as a cynic observed, 'all the hot air could escape'. Similar interference bedevilled G.E. Street when, after the competition, he was invited to build the Law Courts. Barry's son Edward had proposed a grandiose pastiche of his father's Westminster building, which pleased the judges, but Street's more modest design won the day.

The Victoria Tower on Parliament, seen in 1991 (*right*), is under scaffolding during cleaning and restoration work.

BIG BEN AND NELSON'S COLUMN

If there are two tall 'sights' of London which tourists can hardly miss, they are Nelson's column in Trafalgar Square (*right*) and Big Ben, the clock tower on the Houses of Parliament (*above*). Sir Charles Barry laid out the square and, after the 1834 fire which destroyed the medieval Palace of Westminster, he won the competition to design the new Gothic-style Parliament buildings. The bell is named either after Benjamin Caunt, a famous boxer, or Sir Benjamin Hall, the Commissioner of Works at the time it was winched into the tower.

WHITEHALL AND HORSE GUARDS

Right Every year in June, Horse Guards Parade is the
scene of military pageants. Stands are put up around three
sides for the ceremonies of Beating Retreat – a reminder of
a time when drummers gave warning that garrison gates
were about to close – and Trooping the Colour. The latter
is a celebration for the sovereign's official birthday and has
been held here almost continuously since 1895. Queen
Elizabeth II has missed only one parade – in 1955 when a
national rail strike caused its cancellation.

The parade ground, on the site of the Palace of Whitehall's tilt-yard for tournaments, has been used for parades
for centuries. It is overlooked on the north by the
Admiralty and by the pleasant Palladian Horse Guards
building which William Kent and John Vardy built in
1750-8 for the horse and foot guards. Today this is the
headquarters of the officer commanding the combined
forces in London. At the Whitehall entrance, the guard is
changed daily by the Queen's Life Guards, a reminder that
this continues to be the official entrance to St James's Palace
even though somewhat remote from it.

Above In Whitehall the Ministry of Defence buildings,
with river views on the east, have a brash modern effron-
tery compared with nearby Stuart grandeur and subdued
Victorian dignity. They were designed before the Second
World War by Vincent Harris, but not completed until
1959. Mercifully, they are partly screened from Whitehall by the Banqueting House.

GOVERNMENT BUILDINGS AND COUNTY HALL

Left In Parliament Street at the bottom of Whitehall a range of massive late Victorian government offices runs west to St James's Park. Discreet door plates on the buildings facing the park and King Charles Street are seemingly reluctant to announce one of several Treasury buildings in Whitehall. It is almost too complicated to work out the confusion of government offices, but it is interesting to see how one architect – the little-trumpeted J. M. Brydon – found his inspiration in Inigo Jones's 1638 abandoned plan for a magnificent new palace of Whitehall. Jones had wanted a series of quadrangles and a circular courtyard based on the Roman baths of the Emperor Caracalla. This view from the air shows how Brydon achieved Jones's 'Caracella' effect and arranged for courtyards. He also copied Jones's towers with stone domes, one of which is seen here. Looking north-west, the short diagonal façade in the foreground has entrance gates into the circular courtyard, and another facing gateway gives on to King Charles Street and the Foreign Office.

Above In 1892 an anonymous pamphlet, *The Doom of the County Council of London*, satirically prophesied that the administrative headquarters of the Council would become an opulent hotel 'largely patronised by wealthy American visitors'. County Hall had not even been built, but now – seventy years after the London County Council offices were opened in 1922 – it is a brave but deserted mausoleum by Westminster Bridge. Ralph Knott's impressive building, which he hoped would stand comparison with Parliament across the river, became empty in 1986 after the Greater London Council was disbanded. All manner of uses have been proposed, and ironically the favourite plan is to turn it into a luxury hotel – as predicted 100 years ago. But the hotel idea has foundered for lack of finance, and as too much of a gamble.

THE SENATE HOUSE AND CHARING CROSS

Right Spectacular is a mild way to describe the building that has replaced the grimy railway station which for generations stood at Charing Cross. Today's passengers might reasonably expect to find a launching pad to the spheres rather than the same old departure platform for Hither Green. Terry Farrell's 1990 *Star Trek* structure is sufficiently futuristic to be called 'Post-Modern' and is not, of course, just a rail terminus. It has the same number of lines winding out across Hungerford Bridge – with 120,000 commuters using 800 services a day – as there were before. But in addition the new dark glass and grey granite monster, with vast windows overlooking the Thames, has nine floors of vibration-free offices for 3,000 people. At night it looks particularly dramatic.

To subdue reactionary criticisms of this Mighty Wurlitzer of a train-shed, admiring architectural pundits compare the silhouette with the glass-roofed Grand Palais on the Seine; the architect is dubbed a modern-day Vanbrugh for his 'building of unforgettable power'; so-called 'eyebrow' arches on towers are claimed to 'echo' the Georgian river front of Somerset House; and low platform ceilings and 'bulbous globe' lighting are reported to be inspired by Moscow Underground. Posterity has yet to have its say.

Before its antecedents are forgotten in all this hyperbole, it is worth recalling the first station – child of Victorian 'Railway Mania' – which was opened in 1864 and, as befitted a station that was also the gateway to Paris, incorporated a grand hotel built in the French Renaissance style.

Above The administrative Senate House of London University behind the British Museum looks at first glance to be impressive and complete enough in itself. But, started in 1932, Charles Holden's plan was interrupted by the war. He had intended a spine northwards as far as Torrington Square. The air view also reveals the ground plan to be an irregular square.

KING'S CROSS AND VICTORIA

Left Within a few years the wasteland around King's Cross and St Pancras stations will alter dramatically. The new British Library is nearing completion on the corner of Euston Road – to the left of the St Pancras Hotel. An area of grubby charm behind the train-sheds is to be redeveloped. British Rail intend to build a Channel Tunnel terminus at King's Cross for passengers travelling to the North, and there are plans to bring commuter trains from Kent on to new platforms underneath existing lines. Offices and a park alongside the Regent's Canal are envisaged but, in late 1991, pressure groups were resisting even the temporary closure of a small nature park.

Norman Foster's scheme – preferred by British Rail but challenged by another consortium – demands resiting the park and the removal but not the destruction of some Victorian stucco houses. The High Gothic exuberance of St Pancras Hotel will also be preserved. Legend insists that St Pancras is Gilbert Scott's rejected design for the Foreign Office, and the architect hinted at this.

Above 'Southern Railway' proclaims the sign over Victoria Station. This is the entrance to the original and Continental part of the station, the terminus of the London, Chatham and Dover Railway. To its right is the taller baroque frontage of the London, Brighton and South Coast line, a separate, rival station until they amalgamated in 1899. This adjoins the Grosvenor Hotel, a very French-looking building (by J.T. Knowles) with busts of Victorian worthies set in medallions decorating the outside. As at modern Charing Cross, 'air rights' space above the station was filled in the 1980s with a large shopping precinct and offices (visible at the top of the picture).

CLAPHAM JUNCTION

The names of railway stations are sometimes a little arbitrary. Clapham Junction was actually in Battersea when a signal box was put up there in 1839, twenty-four years before the station opened. Perhaps growing Clapham was considered more likely to produce passengers than the scattered houses and farmland then existing at Battersea. Clapham Junction is not so much a station as a district most commuters go through at great speed. At one time, with lines converging on Waterloo and Victoria, and others crossing the river to Kensington, it was the busiest railway junction in the world with over 2,500 passing trains a day. Because there were restrictions on freight crossing the Thames by train, railways companies from other regions opened depots in the Battersea 'tangle', so goods could be transported there not by rail but by road or river.

Clapham Junction is still busy but rival road transport, railway closures and the stream-lining of the seven lines entering the 'tangle' have combined to reduce the number of trains using the junction.

A curious human footnote to the station is the ignominy suffered on a platform by Oscar Wilde. In November 1895 Wilde, during his two-year prison sentence, was transferred from Wandsworth to Reading Gaol. Handcuffed and in prison clothes, he had to wait half-an-hour in the rain at Clapham Junction while a jeering crowd formed round him, and one man spat at him. For a year afterwards, Wilde recalled in *De Profundis*, he wept every day at the same hour for the same space of time.

WATERLOO AND BATTERSEA

Left The snow pattern of railway lines, buffers and signals outside Waterloo Station look like inky streaks in this winter scene in February 1991. Waterloo, like King's Cross, is undergoing a transformation, and a Continental terminus (designed by Nicholas Grimshaw) for Channel Tunnel passengers arriving in London is being built to the south of the station.

Right Battersea Power Station has become a skeleton of its former self. The Colossus of Battersea aroused controversy when Sir Giles Scott's electricity power station was proposed in 1929: the *Architects' Journal* prophesied 'noxious fumes by the ton'. Architectural brickbats followed its opening in 1937. When the two 337-foot chimneys later became four, it was compared to an upturned table and a stranded elephant waving its legs in the air. By 1983, the climate had changed and the building was widely accepted and admired as a marvel of design by people like English Heritage and the Thirties Society, who regarded it as a symbol of the technological era. Just as it was due to be demolished, a preservation order was slapped on it. A competition to find a new use fired the imagination of a leisure park owner. This entrepreneur's proposed £200 million hi-tech entertainment centre ran out of money. The white elephant, waving its legs in the air, lies open to the skies, its future still in doubt in 1991.

Above With the disarming appearance of cooking rings on a vast stove, these circles are, in fact, part of the sewage works in the East London borough of Newham. The works are on the Thames, just to the west of Barking Creek and near the Becton gas works, an area so delapidated in the early 1980s that a film company used it with little alteration and the addition of some bedraggled palm trees to stand in as bomb-damaged Vietnam. The Royal Docks and London City Airport, all part of the docklands redevelopment scheme, lie to the south-west.

Right A mile to the west is a pattern of mortality formed by thousands of graves in the East Ham Jewish Cemetery. The Prayer Hall, looking a little like a seaside pavilion, stands at its centre. The cemetery belongs to United Synagogues, the largest orthodox group in the country, and was opened in 1919 after the Great War and the influenza epidemic filled other Jewish cemeteries in the East End. There are about 40,000 graves, most of first and second generation immigrants who came from Eastern Europe to the East End. In accordance with traditional Jewish custom, only one person is buried in each grave. The inscriptions on the gravestones rarely indicate the importance of the incumbents or how they died, but from sparse information such as 'born Berlin 1926, died October 1940' it is possible to deduce that some immigrant child was killed, possibly by an enemy bomb from his country of origin. Green tombstones are war graves, and members of the Czech Pioneer Corps are buried here.

LORD'S CRICKET GROUND

The quintessentially English game of cricket is the only sport to have a large ground near central London. Lord's Cricket Ground in St John's Wood is not only the home of the MCC (Marylebone Cricket Club); the Middlesex Cricket Club is also based here, sometimes causing confusion about the initials MCC. Lord's is the acknowledged world headquarters of cricket, and until 1969 the MCC was responsible for the laws of the game.

The ground takes its name from Thomas Lord, a Yorkshireman, who first enclosed seven acres of Dorset Square for the game in 1787. When the club moved to St John's Wood in 1813, the turf came too, so that 'the noblemen and gentlemen of the MCC should be able to play on the same footing as before'.

The first Test Match at Lord's was in 1884 – England versus the Australians. Five years later the distinctive stand and club premises (designed by Thomas Verity) were built. Between the twin towers runs the famous Long Room, the hallowed preserve of the gentlemen members who are able to watch the matches from behind the gallery's long windows. The undulations on the revolutionary tent-like white roof (by Michael Hopkins) over the new stand that backs on to St John's Wood Road cannot be appreciated from an overhead angle.

THE OVAL AND WEMBLEY STADIUM

Above Why the Oval? From the air it is clear that it is an accurate description. The Kennington headquarters of the Surrey Cricket Club since 1845 was originally intended and laid out as a residential double crescent or circus, but there was insufficient interest and the Oval was leased to the club by the Duchy of Cornwall estate. The club hosted the first Test Match ever held in England – against the Australians – in 1880, and by tradition the last match in every Test series in England is played here. The huge gasholder, familiar world-wide from broadcast commentaries and to TV spectators, is on the left.

After the Second World War, when the grounds had been set aside for use as a temporary prisoner-of-war camp, alterations were made. More have taken place recently, the brewery which poured in money receiving recognition in the new name – Foster's Oval.

Right Wembley Stadium has been among the best known football grounds in the world for most of this century, but other sports, such as hockey and rugby league are played here. Its size also makes it ideal for the huge crowds attracted by pop concerts. The stadium is part of an all-purpose centre for sports, entertainment and conferences and was originally built for the British Empire Exhibition in 1924. More than 250,000 tons of clay were excavated when the last remnants of a frustrated scheme to give London the equivalent of the Eiffel Tower foundered for lack of money. The stadium was completed four days before the first FA Cup Final at Wembley. The game between Bolton and West Ham attracted over 200,000 spectators, more than double the ground's capacity. Tens of thousands were removed by the police, but this record attendance – on 29 April 1923 – remains unbroken even by such extravagant events as Bob Geldof's charity concert to raise money for Ethiopian famine victims.

THE ROYAL HOSPITAL, CHELSEA

The Royal Hospital, Chelsea, is a residential home for old soldiers, familiar figures in their scarlet coats and campaign medals. One of three such establishments in the British Isles, it was founded by Charles II in imitation of Les Invalides in Paris, and is the only one still used for its original purpose. All the buildings around the Figure Court (centre) and most around the College Court (left) are exactly as built in 1682 to Sir Christopher Wren's designs.

The hospital is still run on the military lines Charles II intended. A governor and a number of senior ex-army officers are in command of six companies of In-Pensioners, whose pillar box red uniforms have scarcely changed since the days of the Duke of Marlborough's 18th-century army. It is part of Chelsea mythology that someone once absently-minded posted a letter in the pocket of one of them. The men live in dormitories and dine each day in the Great Hall (to the

HARRODS

Harrods in the Brompton Road, once a small grocery store, had so expanded since 1849 that by the end of the last century it was already said 'to serve the world'. Spreading over more than four and a half acres today, its fame is world-wide. There is very little that cannot be bought in this versatile shop, which pioneered telephone ordering and free country deliveries. At night, tiny white lights pick out the Edwardian outline of the dome, gables, turrets and exterior walls of the inevitably terracotta building (by Stevens and Munt).

Harrods was one of a number of shops that grew in size towards the end of the 19th century. In 1863, William Whiteley had opened a small drapers in Westbourne Grove, Bayswater, that gradually began to sell jewellery, furs and umbrellas as well as silks and clothing. Whiteley's eventual boast was that he could supply anything 'from a pin to an elephant'. He was followed by such men as Peter Jones in Chelsea and John Barker who, after working for ten years at Whiteley's, set up on his own in Kensington High Street. Charles Derry went into partnership with Toms who sold toys. The Ponting brothers from Gloucestershire became their competitors. These growing stores were rivals, but proximity increased rather than reduced business. Shopping in well-to-do districts as well as the West End became popular and easier with the spread of public transport.

BUCKINGHAM PALACE

This superb vista, challenging Versailles, makes Queen Mary's description of a 'fine wide carriage road' something of an understatement. But it has not always been so. Early in this century the Mall was just a narrow road through St James's Park. The erection of Admiralty Arch and the memorial to Victoria in front of Buckingham Palace turned it into a triumphal route to commemorate the Queen-Empress. Victoria, who made the palace her home in 1837, was the first sovereign to live here, although when it was a modest house George III did come here from Windsor or Kew. On instructions from John Nash, builders enlarged it during the reigns of George IV and William IV. An open forecourt faced the Mall until the east front was built in 1847. The façade was latterly altered, and there are now some 600 rooms. The view (*right*) suggests an invasion of royal privacy, but the Queen's personal apartments are on the far side – and anyway she is not in residence: the Royal Standard is not flying.

In the Queen's Gallery, in the foreground, are some of the fine Royal Collection. The gallery and the Royal Mews (out of view, left) are the only parts of the palace open to the public.

THE VICTORIA MEMORIAL AND CARLTON GARDENS

Left Nine statues, two medallions and two busts are London's outdoor memorials to Queen Victoria, perhaps not excessive for England's longest reigning sovereign. The largest, best known and most elaborate is on the *rond point* in front of Buckingham Palace. The marble statue of the Queen, who looks imperiously down the Mall, is surrounded by symbolic figures, animals and mythical creatures and, for good measure, is surmounted by a gilded winged figure of Victory. The sculptor was Sir Thomas Brock and the memorial's designer was Sir Aston Webb, who in 1913 was responsible for putting the severe front on the palace.

Above Two fine terraces overlooking St James's Park from the north were built on the site of Carlton House, after the Prince Regent's palace on the Mall was demolished in 1827. These houses in Carlton Gardens, the work of Nash in 1830, are mostly occupied by long-established societies and institutions. But their historical past is of rather more interest. The west terrace, seen here, went up on part of a famous garden created over half-a-century earlier by William Kent for Augusta, Princess of Wales. She was the Prince Regent's grandmother and lived in an early version of Carlton House when she came up to town from Kew (page 155). It was after her death in 1772 that George III gave the house to his eldest son, and the Prince spent a fortune transforming it into the legendary palace. Structural defects caused him to dismantle his sumptuous home after he had, in any case, decided Buckingham House would make a better palace. The furnishings from China, enormous quantities of silver and gold plate and paintings remain part of the Royal Collection.

LAMBETH PALACE

Lambeth Palace, the Archbishop of Canterbury's London home on the river, is a fine survival of medieval times. The red brick gatehouse, built in 1490 in the reign of Henry VII, is some sixty years older than the Great Hall, which is seen with the hexagonal lantern. The square Water Tower beyond the hall, and once by the river's edge, dates back to 1432.

Immediately outside the gatehouse is St Mary-at-Lambeth, which has been converted into the Museum of Garden History.

KENSINGTON PALACE

The range of buildings on the east side of Kensington Palace, nearest the camera, are the State Apartments. These rooms, now open to the public, were used by William and Mary, who with Wren's help transformed modest Nottingham House into a palace.

Since the death of George II, the apartments around the three courtyards – the Clock Court, the Princesses' Court and Prince of Wales's Court – have been 'grace and favour' homes granted by the sovereign to relatives. Five branches of the royal family now occupy them.

KENSINGTON GARDENS AND HYDE PARK

Nannies and parents come to Kensington Gardens to play with children. Sir James Barrie once observed that bow-legged children were 'those who had to walk too soon because their father needed the perambulator' to bring large boats to sail on the Round Pond. Children might also be brought to see the statue of Barrie's Peter Pan hidden in the trees. The circular lake in the view on the left was the idea of Queen Caroline, George II's wife. Inspired by the basin conceived by Wren near Hampton Court, she had a pond excavated to the side of Kensington Palace and filled with water in 1728. She also had the River Westbourne dammed, and a chain of small ponds in the valley further to the east were linked to create the Long Water which separates the gardens from Hyde Park.

Kensington Gardens are seen here from three angles. The picture on the left looks south to Museumland. *Above, right*, is the Long Water which has Hyde Park on its east side. At the top of this view is an Italianate garden containing fountains and Queen Anne's Alcove designed by Wren. Other ornamental features in imitation of the Petit Trianon at Versailles are said to have been suggested by the Prince Consort. The third view (*bottom, right*) shows more of Kensington Gardens and Hyde Park south of Bayswater Road terraces.

HYDE PARK

The Serpentine in Hyde Park is invisible except in outline under snow and ice in the upper left view, and glittering in summer sunlight, above. Like the Round Pound, the Serpentine was also Queen Caroline's idea. Working with her protégé, William Kent, she employed 200 men to construct the great ornamental expanse of water as an extension of the Long Water. Kent, the most fashionable landscape architect of his day, had denounced long canals, stating that Nature disliked a straight line, so the Queen had the outline curved to give a 'natural' look. George II believed the Queen was paying for the extensive alterations in Kensington Gardens and Hyde Park out of her own pocket. After her death, he discovered that with the connivance of her friend Sir Robert Walpole, the Prime Minister, the Treasury had footed the bill.

The tree-lined rectangle of grass lined with trees and overlooked by the tall tower of Knightsbridge Barracks (designed by Sir Basil Spence) is the site of Sir Joseph Paxton's Crystal Palace for the Great Exhibition. During the 141 days of 1851 that the great glass structure was open, over six million people came to see the 'Works of Industry of all Nations'. On the opening day alone between 500,000 and 700,000 people assembled in the Park, and there were some 25,000 visitors to the building. Some of the foundations are said to remain hidden under the ground and although they cannot be seen here the Coalbrookdale Gates, which were in the exhibition, remain a visual reminder of the Crystal Palace. They are in Kensington Gardens, facing the end of the South Carriage Drive.

Parallel with the drive and the Crystal Palace site, beside the Serpentine, is Rotten Row, a riding track for exercising horses. The name is derived from the *route du roi*, the road William III took on his way from Westminster to Kensington Palace. Because highwaymen lurked in the park, the King's Road was the first street in London to have lighting.

HYDE PARK AND THE SERPENTINE

Above Like some magic emblem the double star in Lovers'
Walk in Hyde Park encloses a fountain, on which dancing
Bacchanalian figures represent the Joy of Life. This statue
by T.B. Huxley-Jones was unveiled in 1963 after the older
classical Boy and a Dolphin was removed to Regent's
Park. It is one of many fountains and statues in London
paid for by a fund set up in memory of the artist Sigismund
Goetze by his wife.

Right More magic – and certainly an entrancing and
mysterious pattern – is suggested by this little island off the
north shore of the Serpentine. Crossing into Hyde Park
from his small house in the Bayswater Road, Barrie could
have fancifully imagined this as a setting for one of his
plays – another Island That Wants To Be Visited, a Never
Never Land planted with a Wood of What Might Have
Been. To add colour to whimsy, blue and yellow boats,
tied up and catching the tip of the sun in the dark waters,
resemble the tail of an exotic oriental kite.

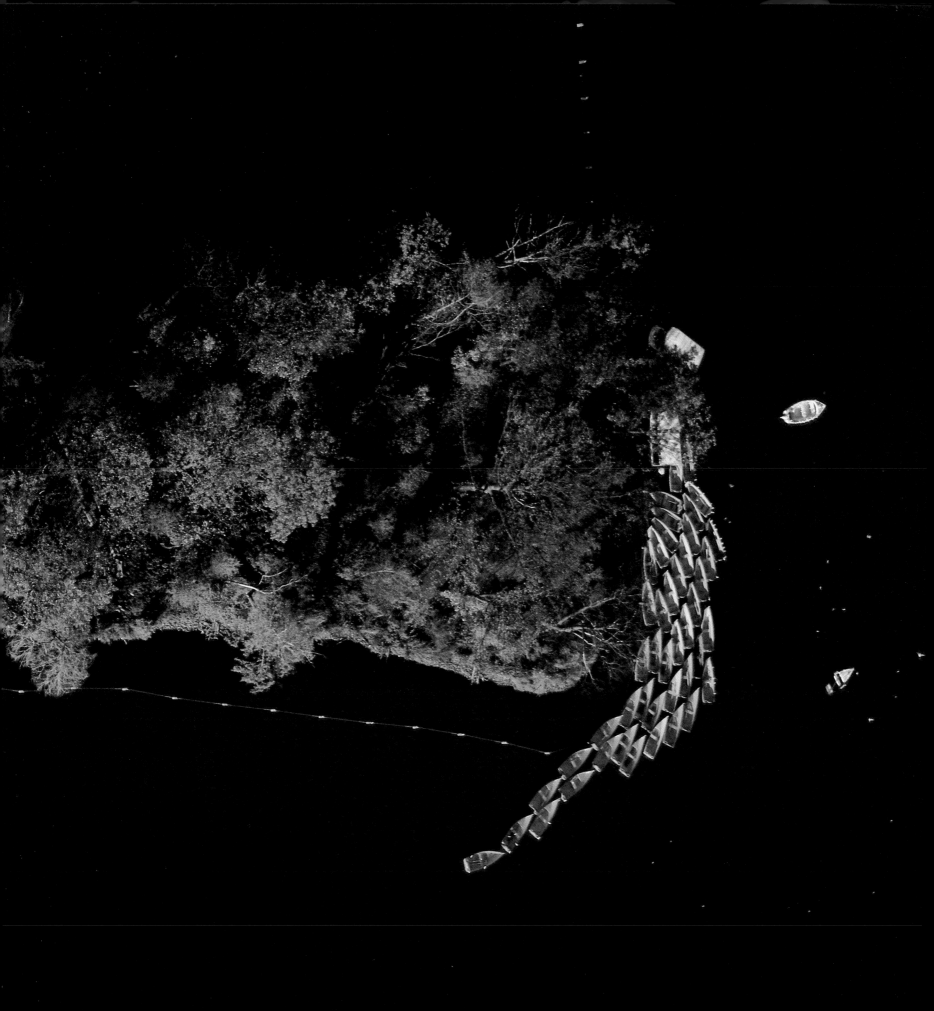

REGENT'S PARK

John Nash's proposal to build terraces of elegant houses around the new Regent's Park in Marylebone coincided with the London building boom after the Napoleonic Wars. They have survived brilliantly, and these three views give some idea of the peripheral arrangement. On the left is the south-west side of the park, and on the far edge of the picture Sussex Place overlooks the boating lake. With cupolas, curved wings and fifty-six Corinthian columns seemingly added for luck, this is not what people generally associate with Nash; and the terrace was much criticised when it was built in 1822. General preference is for the classical glories of Hanover Terrace, next to it, with porticos, pediments and arcades in the admired classical style. Both terraces may also be compared, above right, viewed from the opposite direction. Bedford College, in the foreground, was built in 1903 at the sacrifice of South Villa, a charming Regency house. Happily surviving is the large cream villa seen in the foreground of the snow view, right. This is the Holme, designed by Nash's pupil, Decimus Burton, when he was eighteen. The circle encloses Queen Mary's Gardens, notable for their roses and the Open Air Theatre where, bravely defying the weather, Shakespeare is performed in summer.

THE ZOO AND REGENT'S PARK

Left Nice weather for polar bears. Somewhere in the frozen triangle in Regent's Park is the
London Zoo, where jungle animals are grateful for central heating and arctic ones revel in the
snow. New, plausibly more attractive and comfortable homes have been built for an increasing number of animals since the Zoo gardens were laid out in 1828.

SURBURBAN SPRAWL

Driving past them is not the same. Looking down on all these chimneys, roofs and trim gardens it is impossible not to wonder how the seemingly endless streets ever came about. The answer is that rows of uniform housing were started at the turn-of-the-century and continued remorselessly in the 1920s and 1930s to accommodate London's fast-growing population.

In the medieval city, and until well into the 19th century, shopkeepers and their staffs lived where they worked. They occupied the upper floors over their shops and workplaces or else they lived close by. This pattern gradually changed in mid-Victorian times. More and more private houses in the City were turned into commercial premises. Prosperity, the spread of the railways and the population boom caused an exodus into the suburbs. Crowded tenements were deserted for endless ranks of terraced houses in districts increasingly served by trains. In acres that were transformed into a surburban sprawl, small gardens became the only reminders of vanished countryside.

Many suburbs maintained their individuality as villages and small towns, until ribbon-development along arterial roads in the new century linked them up into an amorphous mass. With the First World War building came to a halt, and this led to a demand which, starting in 1922, resulted in about 700,000 houses being built between the wars. Some were council houses, but the great majority were private houses put up by speculative builders. Especially in the north-west, the demand was for sizeable, semi-detached and detached houses. Names like Dunroamin and Mon Repose appeared on gates everywhere, along with Tudor gables, bay windows and front doors with stained-glass panels.

Above South London was inclined to be less expensive than elsewhere, and in suburbs which grew up around Sidcup modest £500 houses could be obtained for a £5 deposit, and an 8 shilling a week repayment. 'Brick-built throughout', read a reassuring Mitcham hoarding, with the tempting afterthought 'Nearly Every House has a Garage Space'. In well-established Victorian suburbs, room for building was harder to find, and the above view shows how new avenues, crescents and a modern housing block had to seek haphazard places in surroundings of older, larger buildings and paths.

In contrast, Ilford (*right*) conforms to the prototype suburban sprawl of hardly varying houses in strictly regimented rows. Surprisingly, these houses are older than they might appear. Off Ilford Lane, which runs diagonally across the centre, side-streets have names like Khartoum, Madras and Bengal, their Imperial flavour revealing them as part of a late 19th-century development.

BAYSWATER AND LITTLE VENICE

Above The tall spire on Christ Church, Lancaster Gate, appears part of a very distinguished church. This it was in Victorian days, when it was known as the 'thousand pound church' because it was not unusual for £1,000 or more to be collected at a single Sunday morning service. The prosperous professional-class residents of Bayswater put silver in the plate for the poor and their less fortunate neighbours in Shepherd's Bush and Paddington. Unfortunately the church itself fell on hard times, and dry rot led to the demolition of everything except the spire in 1978. What appear to be distinctive buttresses are in fact concrete imitations above an ill-advised block of flats named Spire House.

Right Little Venice is the inspired name coined by an estate agent in the 1950s for this pleasant part of Paddington. Fortunately the modern Westway Flyover (bottom, right) has not unduly disrupted the quasi-Venetian tranquillity. The houses on the edge of the triangle of water at the start of the Regent's Canal – many with charming gardens – make this one of London's unexpected oases. After entering the basin under Westbourne Road Terrace, the canal runs eastwards along tree-lined Blomfield Avenue and goes into several tunnels before emerging to curve round Regent's Park (top, right). This completed the last link in the Grand Union Canal between Birmingham and the Thames at Limehouse.

Maida Vale, immediately to the north, was spaciously laid out in the middle of the 19th century with large houses and elegant terraces which attracted prosperous residents. Who today would know that the district took its name from the Battle of Maida, a British victory over the French in 1805? At the top of the view is Lord's Cricket Ground, and beyond it Primrose Hill.

REGENT'S PARK AND BAYSWATER

Above Bayswater was sometimes known as Tyburnia in the last century. A residential district north of Hyde Park (previously seen on page 140), the area was developed between 1807-40 on the Bishop of London's estate, which lay west of the gallows at Tyburn. This view looking west shows the less definable part of Bayswater behind the Bayswater Road. While never as fashionable as Mayfair or Belgravia, the terraces were occupied by well-to-do middle class business people. Some houses suffered bomb damage and were demolished, only to be replaced by the Church Commissioners whose redevelopment has not been outstanding.

The Serpentine, which separates Hyde Park from Kensington Gardens, is visible top left. In this light the Round Pond looks more like a milk pond than an ornamental lake.

Left The arc of colonnaded houses at the entrance to Regent's Park is Park Crescent. This is half of a projected circus intended by John Nash to be the third and final circus on the grand thoroughfare from Carlton House to the new palace – never realised – which he planned in the park for the Prince Regent. Piccadilly Circus and Oxford Circus (pages 66-7) were completed, but the builder of the circus went bankrupt. The other half of his circus – across the Marylebone Road – became an open 'square'. The centre grey building on the far side of Park Square is the surviving façade of a lost entertainment – the Diorama. Behind it the out-line of the circular auditorium built by Nash and Augustus Pugin the Elder for Louis Daguerre. A forerunner of the cinema, the 'Palace of Light' opened in 1823. As the auditorium revolved through a 73-degree turn, audiences saw romantic landscapes and architectural interiors projected on to two translucent screens – bigger than any cinema screen today. An uncertain future awaits the last Daguerre diorama left in the world.

WEMBLEY AND PRIMROSE HILL

Right Primrose Hill has a poetic name, but one wonders when primroses were last picked there. From the air, this knoll with fine views south over London is flattened out and loses its pleasant contours. It is not easy to pick out the 200-foot high summit of the hill – where people exercise dogs and take picnics – overlooking Regent's Park and the triangle beyond the canal which is the Zoo. Primroses or not, there are clumps of trees scattered over the hill, among them an oak planted to commemorate Shakespeare's 400th birthday, a replacement for one planted a hundred years earlier by the actor Samuel Phelps.

Primrose Hill, granted to Eton College by Henry VI, was leased by the college for building in the 1820s, but before the land was seriously encroached it was acquired by the Crown. The names of some of the roads in the foreground retain Eton associations. Buildings have nibbled into the land to the east of Avenue Road that runs up to Swiss Cottage, and the rather inelegant corrugated roof covers a reservoir.

Above To the right of the Northern Line by Wembley Park station, and half a mile from Wembley Stadium, are interconnecting blocks of flats. With the zig-zag pattern touched by early morning sun, Chalk Hill Estate has a look of idyllic tranquillity. But the estate (designed in the 1960s for Brent Council) is not quite as peaceful as it appears. Walkways connecting the blocks, built in the hope of enhancing community spirit, have – as in other parts of London – led to crime and petty disorder. In the far distance is Harrow on the Hill and Harrow School; and the whole of this part of north-west London is dotted with parks and sports grounds. Shouts of 'Heel, School!' and 'Play up, Wasps!' fill the Saturday afternoon air.

RICHMOND AND BLACKHEATH

Above In Richmond the 'battle of the styles' has been largely won by the architect Quinlan Terry. His Neo-Classical Revival redevelopment of the riverside site by the Georgian bridge has considerable local approval, and the Prince of Wales has acclaimed the 'harmony and proportion' of the houses and offices. Others criticise it as self-consciously pastiche Georgian. And it is true that Terry incorporated an uninhibited variety of classical orders. No fewer than ten different column designs appear among the 16th-century Italian and 18th-century English-style buildings alongside restored Victorian fabric. Cupolas, gateways and decorative detail add to the overall Palladian effect.

Richmond-upon-Thames, a favourite residence of the Tudor sovereigns, became a country retreat for courtiers and City merchants. The Green (left), where Henry VII held tournaments at the end of the 15th century, has continued its associations with entertainment. David Garrick and Edmund Kean appeared at Richmond Theatre. The present theatre on the Green, recently restored, is late-Victorian. Kean, who was the lessee of the Georgian theatre, lived in Richmond, as do a number of modern entertainers.

Right For a village only seven miles from central London, Blackheath has a surprisingly country atmosphere. The main triangle of shops lies in a dip called Tranquil Vale on the southern boundary of flat open heathland. The heath stretches from All Saints Church across the main London to Dover road, which means that – with Greenwich Park – there is open country almost down to the Thames. The heath is framed by large Georgian and Victorian houses, most of which are still residential. Like Richmond, Blackheath has two Tudor palaces not far away – Greenwich and Eltham – which provide an additional historical flavour.

HAMPSTEAD VILLAGE AND HAMPSTEAD HEATH

Hampstead is another village which has managed to retain its individuality. Even trendy boutiques and restaurants have not destroyed the atmosphere of an artistic and literary past which has continued into the present. Fine 18th- and 19th-century houses are attractive, half-hidden features of alleys and courtyards off Heath Street, which can be seen (*above, left*) winding north from the village to Whitestone Pond and Hampstead Heath. At the centre of the view (*left* and *above, left*) is the steeple of Christ Church in Hampstead Square. The walled garden, lawn and yew trees at Fenton House, a red brick William and Mary house, are also visible (bottom left, *left*). One of the earliest and largest houses in the village, and now containing a collection of early musical instruments, it is owned by the National Trust.

The grounds of Kenwood, seen in the far distance (*above, right*) were added to the heath when Edward Guinness, the 1st Earl of Iveagh, left the house and a valuable art collection to the nation in 1927. Two years earlier, when plans to build on the woodland had been mooted, the Earl had intervened and bought the estate in order to preserve the seat of the Mansfield family, which Robert Adam had transformed into an example of an 18th-century gentlemen's residence. From Kenwood's high position above the woods and ponds on the heath, there is a fine view of the City.

WHITESTONE POND AND CRYSTAL PALACE

Above Springs with medicinal qualities brought society to Hampstead in the late 17th century, and chalybeate water found in Well Walk was sold in nearby Flask Walk. Ponds, of which the Whitestone (above) is one of the smallest, are also a pleasant feature of the heath. This great open space, comprising some 800 acres of wood and rolling fields, was preserved for the public by an Act of Parliament in 1871. Charles Dickens, at one time a regular walker on the Heath, frequently wrote about it in his novels. Once, forsaking work on *Pickwick Papers* for a few hours, he sent a note to his friend and biographer John Forster to ask if he felt disposed 'to muffle yourself up, and start off with me for a good brisk walk over Hampstead Heath? I know a good 'ouse there where we can have a red-hot chop for dinner, and a glass of good wine'. Forster later recalled that it led 'to our first experience of Jack Straw's Castle, memorable for many happy meetings in coming years'. The inn that Dickens and Forster knew was badly damaged during the Second World War, and replaced by the present white weather-board building (top, right).

Right The BBC television transmitter is a landmark in Sydenham, an area better known as Crystal Palace because the 1851 Great Exhibition building was brought here from Hyde Park. From the air the ground-plan of the huge glass and iron-ribbed building can be visualised sited between the road on the right and the steps leading down to the grounds. The designer, Sir Joseph Paxton, had a nearby house on Sydenham Hill. The Crystal Palace was destroyed by fire on 30 November 1936.

HAMPTON COURT

From this angle, the flamboyant Tudor parts of Hampton Court Palace can be distinguished from the more restrained classical renaissance State Apartments which Sir Christopher Wren re-built around the Fountain Court 200 years later. The turrets, towers and moulded chimneys near the west front and the Base Court are part of the magnificent house Cardinal Wolsey built early in the reign of Henry VIII. Wolsey, whose household numbered almost 500, entertained lavishly and always kept 280 rooms prepared for guests. Their furnishings were far more luxurious than any royal palace, and the King and Catherine of Aragon were greatly impressed when they came on visits. In an attempt to regain favour when he saw the threat of downfall, the Cardinal presented his home to the King, who immediately began to enlarge it. He was so impatient for the Great Hall (centre) to be completed that the craftsmen worked round the clock and by candlelight after dark. During the year that Henry waited for his divorce from Catherine, Anne Boleyn was constantly with the King at Hampton Court and accompanied him on hunts on the estate.

Every sovereign from Henry VIII to George II lived at Hampton Court – with the exception of James II. Among them, the imprint left by William and Mary is strongest. They required a more modern palace, and Wren demolished some of Henry VIII's apartments to make way for more homely suites.

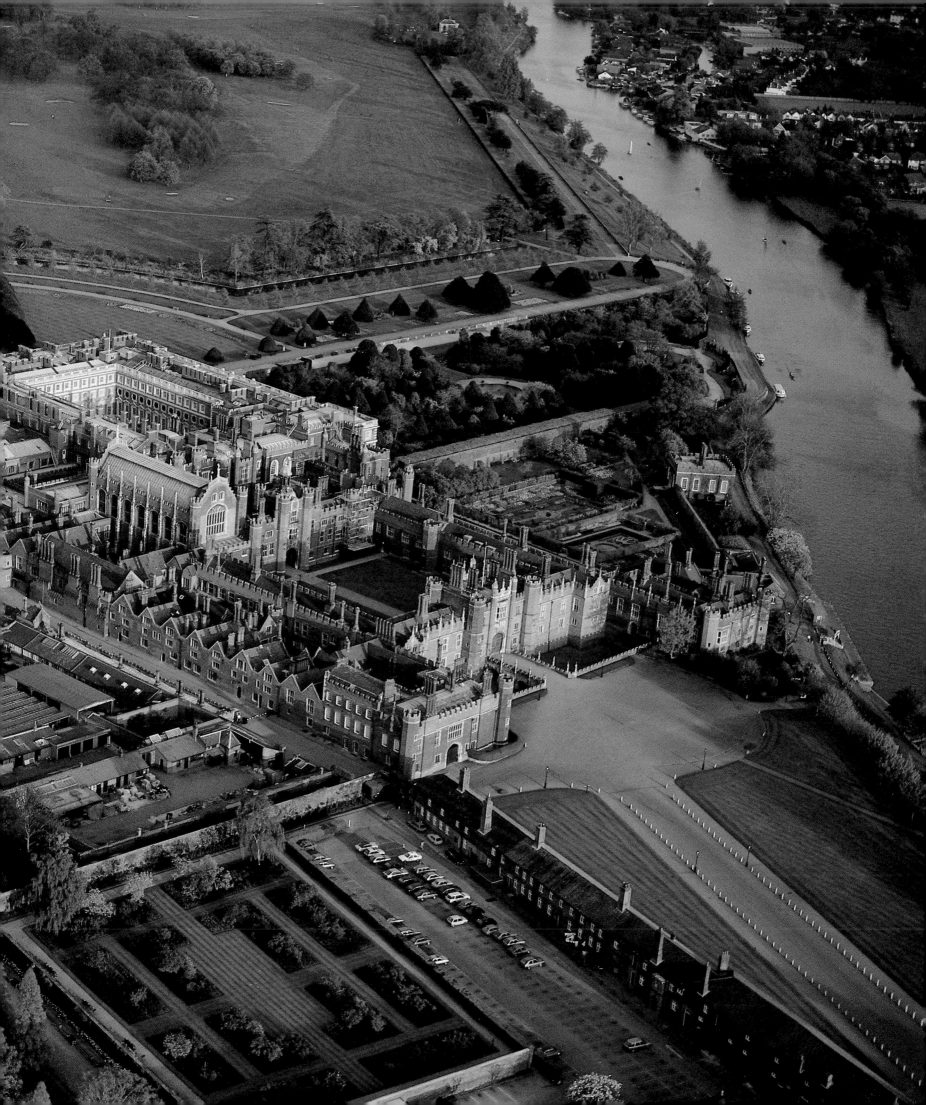

HAMPTON COURT AND KEW

Left Although he had palaces all along the river from Greenwich to Richmond, the estate at Hampton Court, lyrically described as 'meads forever crown'd with flowers' and 'more like unto a paradise than any earthly habitation', greatly delighted Henry VIII. Before Wolsey's downfall he often strolled by the fishponds and fountains, his arm thrown across the Cardinal's shoulders. In the first year that he owned Hampton Court he planted a flower garden, kitchen garden and two orchards. Walks flanked with gilded heraldic beasts were laid out. What is now the Privy Garden, running south to the Thames, was named after Anne Boleyn.

The Tudor gardens were, however, modest compared to those that came later. The semi-circular Great Fountain Garden, with obelisks of yews, was created by Charles II, as were the three avenues of limes that radiate from it. The Long Water canal provided the gardens with a supply of water – for which centuries of gardeners have been grateful and which firemen were able to use to save the palace when a fire threatened to engulf it in 1986. The square red brick building on the river's edge west of the Privy Garden is the Banqueting House, built for William III in 1700.

Right The Royal Botanic Gardens at Kew (see page 156).

KEW GARDENS

Credit for the Royal Botanic Gardens at Kew largely belongs to Augusta, Princess of Wales. Her husband Frederick's strained relationship with his father George II meant the couple were not welcome at St James's Palace or Hampton Court, so subsequently they spent a great deal of time at the White House at Kew. The Prince's mother, Queen Caroline, had a house nearby, on land that had belonged to Richmond Palace; and her love of gardening was inherited by her children, especially Frederick, who called in William Kent to restore the house and to lay out the grounds. After Frederick's death in 1751, Augusta continued the work, extending the landscaping and employing Sir William Chambers as her architectural advisor. A few magnificent trees planted by the Princess still stand, as do several of Chambers's 18th-century buildings, among them the Temple of Arethusa and the Pagoda. The Palm House (*above*) disputes with the Great Pagoda (not visible) the title for the best known building at Kew. It was the first of two great Victorian glasshouses designed for the gardens. The architect Decimus Burton had already cut his teeth on the problem some years earlier, when his practical help had been sought by the 6th Duke of Devonshire at the time he and his gardener Joseph Paxton embarked on the Great Conservatory at Chatsworth. The Palm House, with sheets of curving glass, was intentionally built by the lake so the ribs and beams would be reflected in the water.

The first plants put in on completion in 1848 were examples of a giant palm which had been enclosed for twenty years in brickwork half a mile away. To move the largest roots – weighing 17 tons – engineers had to use tackle before they could be transported on rollers. During recent major restoration work on the Palm House the plants had to be removed, and a similar task faced the gardeners when the building was finished in 1988.

THE PALM HOUSE AT KEW

The Palm House (*above*) disputes with the Great Pagoda (not visible) the title for the best known building at Kew. It was the first of two great Victorian glasshouses designed for the gardens. The architect Decimus Burton had already cut his teeth on the problem some years earlier, when his practical help had been sought by the 6th Duke of Devonshire at the time he and his gardener Joseph Paxton embarked on the Great Conservatory at Chatsworth. The Palm House, with sheets of curving glass, was intentionally built by the lake so the ribs and beams would be reflected in the water.

The first plants put in on completion in 1848 were examples of a giant palm which had been enclosed for twenty years in brickwork half a mile away. To move the largest roots – weighing 17 tons – engineers had to use tackle before they could be transported on rollers. During recent major restoration work on the Palm House the plants had to be removed, and a similar task faced the gardeners when the building was finished in 1988.

Twelve years after the Palm House was completed, the increasing number of large shrubs and trees in various conservatories necessitated the building of another large frost-free house if the plants were to survive. Decimus Burton's 1860 design for the Temperate House (*opposite*) was in five sections – a high central hall, two octagons and two rectangular houses – but the wings were not completed until the end of the century. Glittering in the surrounding dusk, they both resemble fairytale palaces.

SYON

Syon House has an enviable position. It looks directly across the river to Kew Gardens. And Kew faces Syon. The crenellated house is the climax of a view from the Palm House – the idea of the landscape gardener W. S. Nesfield. When the great conservatory was planned, he recommended that one of three vistas radiating from the west door should take the eye immediately to the oddly 'Gothick' facade of the Duke of Northumberland's house. During recent restoration Syon was given a warm cream stucco finish, which softened the austere exterior that had caused John Betjeman to comment: 'You'd never guess the battlemented house contained such wonders as there are inside it.' Betjeman was referring to the riotious decoration that Robert Adam conjured in the ornate state rooms.

Rather too far away to be seen in detail is the lion statue on the east front of Syon, which was formerly on Northumberland House, the Percy family home in the Strand (demolished in 1874). That lion had a rebellious past. When it was in the Strand, with a dominating position looking towards Trafalgar Square, one of the dukes, who thought he had been slighted at Court, is said to have turned the lion around so that its raised tail faced St James's Palace. Anyway, honour has now been fully restored: at Syon the lion politely faces far-off St James's.

Henry Percy, the 9th Earl of Northumberland who was nicknamed 'Wizard', was granted the lease of Syon by Elizabeth I in 1593. When a distant kinsman became involved in the Gunpowder Plot to kill James I, the Earl was confined to the Tower from where, impervious to imprisonment, he set about organising the building of the 'pepperpot' lodges on the main drive.

158

BLACKHEATH FAIR

Scattered like so many brightly wrapped bon-bons, the funfair sideshows are ready for Bank Holiday pleasures. This might be any number of places around London, but here the whirli-gigs and booths are on Blackheath, where people have come for centuries to knock down coco-nuts and, on one occasion, to wonder at a two-headed woman. The fairground folk are still sleeping in their caravans, but later the hurdy-gurdy music will pierce the night air. Let joy be unconfined! This carnival view makes a perfect farewell to London from the air.